The Critical Attitude and the History of International Law

International Legal Theory and Practice

Volumes published in this Brill Research Perspectives title are listed at *brill.com/rplt*

The Critical Attitude and the History of International Law

By

Jean d'Aspremont

BRILL

LEIDEN | BOSTON

This paperback book edition is simultaneously published as issue 1.3 2018, of *International Legal Theory and Practice*, DOI:10.1163/24522058-01030003.

Library of Congress Control Number: 2019946943

Typeface for the Latin, Greek, and Cyrillic scripts: "Brill". See and download: brill.com/brill-typeface.

ISBN 978-90-04-41162-3 (paperback)
ISBN 978-90-04-41163-0 (e-book)

This book is printed on acid-free paper and produced in a sustainable manner.

Printed by Printforce, the Netherlands

Contents

The Critical Attitude and the History of International Law 1
Jean d'Aspremont
Abstract 1
Keywords 1
1 Markers, Periodization, Causal Sequencing, *effet du réel* and the Writing of Historical Narratives 7
2 The Rise of Disciplinary Histories in International Law 14
3 The 'Historical Turn' and the Burgeoning of Critical Histories 25
4 The Continuous Complacency of Contemporary Critical Histories 32
5 The Impossibility of Critical Historiography and the Idea of Radical Historical Critique 39
6 Concluding Remarks 47
Bibliography 52

The Critical Attitude and the History of International Law

Jean d'Aspremont
Sciences Po Law School and University of Manchester
jean.daspremont@sciencespo.fr

Abstract

This article questions the critical attitude that is informing the critical histories that have been flourishing since the 'historical turn' in international law. It makes the argument that the 'historical turn' falls short of being radically critical as the abounding critical histories which have come to populate the international literature over the last decades continue to be orchestrated along the very lines set by the linear historical narratives which they seek to question and disrupt. This article argues that the critical histories must move beyond a mere historiographical attitude and promotes radical historical critique in order to unbridle disciplinary imagination.

Keywords

history of international law – historiography – legal theory – historical turn – radical historical critique – Hayden White – critical theory – linearity – progress narrative

Any discipline needs a history. Disciplinary history is indispensable for the legitimacy and acceptability of the truth-claims that regulate interpretation and discourses within the discipline.[1] Disciplinary history is also instrumental in the self-awareness of those actors constituting the discipline that they are agents of a disciplinary project. From this perspective, it can be argued

1 Keith Jenkins, Re-thinking History (Routledge, 2003), at 39 ("History is a discourse, a language game; within it, 'truth' and similar expressions are devices to open, regulate and shut down interpretations. Truth acts as a censor – it draws the line"). As far as international law is concerned, see gen. J. d'Aspremont, *International Law as a Belief System* (CUP, 2017).

 | DOI:10.1163/9789004411630_002

that international law did not constitute a discipline until the end of the 19th century, that is until international lawyers consciously embarked on the systematic writing of a history of international law and acquired historical self-consciousness.

It is submitted at this preliminary stage that, since the end of the 19th century and the consolidation of international law as a discipline, international lawyers do not only have historical self-consciousness whereby they understand and situate themselves as agent of a disciplinary project but also are historians of sorts. If one understands historicization as an intellectual process meant to provide the past with form and meaning intelligible in the present,[2] international lawyers, in the many activities in which they are engaged, are constantly historicizing.[3] In fact, retrieving, reconstructing, and giving meaning to past texts, doctrines, concepts, and practices for the sake of the present constitutes a central component in the making of international legal discourses.[4] Whether in practice or scholarship, ploughing in past texts, doctrines, concepts, and practices and organizing them in a meaningful way[5] has long been a necessary step in the making of legal arguments, certainly since the 'modernization'

2 Michael S Roth defines history as "a way of putting historical events together into a meaningful whole. See Michael S Roth, 'Foreword: "All You've Got is History"' in Hayden White, *Metahistory. The Historical Imagination in the 19th-Century Europe* (JHU Press, 2014) ix.

3 Anne Orford, 'On international legal method' [2013] 1 London Review of International Law 166, 172 and 175 ("After all, as lawyers, particularly those of us with common law backgrounds, we are trained in the art of making meaning move across time"); Anne Orford, 'International Law and the Limits of History' in W Werner and others (eds), *The Law of International Lawyers: Reading Martti Koskenniemi* (CUP 2015) 297; Thomas Kleinlein, 'International Legal Thought: Creation of a Tradition and the Potential of Disciplinary Self-Reflection' in Giuliana Ziccardi Capaldo, *The Global Community: Yearbook of International Law and Jurisprudence 2016* (OUP 2016) 811, 812; See also Matthew Craven, 'The Invention of a Tradition: Westlake, The Berlin Conference and the Historicisation of International Law' in Luigi Nuzzo and Miloš Vec, *Constructing International Law: The Birth of a Discipline* (Klostermann 2012) 4. Kate Purcell, 'Faltering at the Critical Turn to History: 'Juridical Thinking' in International Law and Genealogy as History, Critique, and Therapy' (2016) Jean Monnet Working Paper Series, JMWP 02/15, 13–15. It is interesting to note that such claim has been made in relation to philosophy as well, for instance by Hegel. On this point, see T Rockmore, 'Hegel' in Aviezer Tucker (ed), *A Companion to the Philosophy of History and Historiography* (Wiley-Blackwell 2011) 468, 474. See the remarks of M Koskenniemi, 'Epilogue' in W Werner and others, *The Law of International Lawyers. Reading Martti Koskenniemi* (CUP 2017) 406–407.

4 For this reason, it has been argued that the distinction between law and history is a modern invention. See Anne Orford, 'The Past as Law of History? The Relevance of Imperialism for Modern International Law' (2012) U of Melbourne Legal Studies Research Paper 600, 8 <https://papers.ssrn.com/sol3/papers.cfm?abstract_id=2090434> accessed 14 June 2018.

5 Michael S Roth 'Foreword: "All You've Got is History"' in Hayden White, *Metahistory. The Historical Imagination in the 19th-Century Europe* (JHU Press, 2014) ix.

of international law. In fact, it is probably the formalization of a 'doctrine of sources'[6] that most decisively entrenched historicization in the making of international legal discourses.[7] In that sense, it can be argued that, since the end of the 19th century, international lawyers are not only agents of a disciplinary project endowed with historical self-awareness. They also are seasoned historians of past texts, doctrines, concepts, and practices.[8] This disciplinary trait remains conspicuous in contemporary international legal scholarship and practice.

International lawyers have been portrayed so far as being endowed with historical self-consciousness and being seasoned historians of past texts, doctrines, concepts, and practices. An important clarification is warranted. That international lawyers are *historians* and endowed with historical self-consciousness does not mean that they are *historiographers* of international law.[9] Said differently, the fact that international lawyers have long been

6 For some remarks on the modern character of the sources doctrine, See Thomas Skouteris, 'The Sources of International Law: Tales of Progress' [2000] Hague Yrbk Intl L 11, 11–17; D Kennedy, 'The Sources of International Law' (1987) 2 (1) American University International Law Review 1. See Jean d'Aspremont, 'Bindingness' in J d'Aspremont and S Singh (eds), *Fundamental Concepts for International Law: The Construction of a Discipline* (2015) (Elgar 2016, forthcoming) <https://ssrn.com/abstract=2690155> Accessed 14 June 2018.

7 In the same vein, Rose Parfitt, 'The Spectre of Sources' [2014] 25 European Journal of International Law 297, 298 ("The classical doctrine of sources, as it emerged in the 19th century, eventually to be codified in Article 38(1) of the ICJ Statute, leaves no doubt as to the historical character of international law's claim to authority and legitimacy – of its claim to be law").

8 Such aphorisms are common in international legal literature. It is nowadays common to say, not without a great deal of oversimplification, that all international law are realists (See H Cohen, 'Are We (Americans) All International Legal Realists Now?' in Chiara Giorgetti and Guglielmo Verdirame (eds), *Concepts on International Law in Europe and the United States* (Cambridge University Press, Forthcoming); University of Georgia School of Law Legal Studies Research Paper 2017–23; Dean Rusk International Center Research Paper 2017–07 <https://ssrn.com/abstract=3025616> Accessed 14 June 2018), formalists (see Jean d'Aspremont, International Lawyers and Legal Forms: Transatlantic Denials Forthcoming in Chiara Giorgetti & Guglielmo Verdirame (eds), *Concepts on International Law in Europe and the United States* (Cambridge University Press, 2018)), critics (see Jean d'Aspremont, 'Martti Koskenniemi, the Mainstream, and Self-Reflectivity' [2016] 29 Leiden Journal of International Law. Accessed 15 June 2018 at <https://ssrn.com/abstract=2718846>.

9 Jenkins notes the interchangeable use of history and historiography in the English language. He regrets the ambiguity of English because the term history does not sufficiently distinguish between history "as that which has been written/recorded about the past" and the past history. In English, history covers both. Hence, it would be better to use "historiography" to refer to the writing of historians about the past. See Keith Jenkins, *Re-thinking History* (Routledge 2003) 7. In contrast, E H H Carr promotes an approach to history that makes it primarily historiographical. See E H H Carr, *What is History?* (2nd ed, CUP 1987) 22 ("when

engaged in the creation of discourses about the past to give the latter a form and a meaning intelligible in the present (*historicization*) does not entail that they have similarly been well-versed in discoursing and theorizing about the specific forms and the meanings provided to the past and the way in which such a past is created (*historiography*).[10]

This distinction between historicization and historiography allows one to capture and better describe a change in the discipline of international law in the last two decades. It is argued here that whilst international lawyers' historical consciousness and historicizing activities have been witnessed as early as the end of the 19th century, historiographical consciousness is a much more recent aptitude among international lawyers. Indeed, according to a common disciplinary narrative heard these days, international lawyers started, in the last two decades, to discourse and theorize about the specific forms and the meanings which their common histories of international law have provided to the past and the way in which such a past has been created. This growth of historiographical consciousness in international legal studies is what is commonly referred in the international legal literature as the 'historical turn',[11] which according to a now common disciplinary narrative, is said to have occurred approximately two decades ago.[12] From the perspective of the above-mentioned distinction between historization and historiography, this so-called 'historical turn' can be understood as a historiographical turn. It marks, not the historical self-consciousness of international lawyers or their historicizing activities, but an upsurge of scholarly works in historiography of the discipline as well as a dramatic rise of interest for critical discoursing and theorizing about the specific forms and meanings given to the past by international

we take up a work of history, our first concern should be not with the facts which it contains but with the historian who wrote it"). Compare with the more generic uses of these notions as the one adopted in the *Companion to the Philosophy of History and Historiography*. See Aviezer Tucker, 'Introduction' in Aviezer Tucker (ed), *A Companion to the Philosophy of History and Historiography* (Wiley-Blackwell 2011), 2.

10 Comp. Keith Jenkins, *On 'What is History'. From Carr and Elton to Rorty and White* (Roultledge 1995) 16. For Keith Jenkins, historiography "theorises both the notion of 'the past' and the 'writing-up' of it".

11 On the turn to history in contemporary international legal scholarship see M Craven, 'Theorizing the Turn to History in International Law', in A Orford and F Hoffmann (eds), *The Oxford Handbook of the Theory of International Law* (OUP 2016), 21–37; see also G Galindo, 'Martti Koskenniemi and the Historiographical Turn in International Law' [2005] 16 European Journal of International Law 539.

12 This watershed moment is often associated with the publication of Martti Koskenniemi's *Gentle Civilizer of Nations* (Cambridge University Press 2001).

lawyers and the way in which such past is written.[13] Before that, international lawyers, we are told, were the complacent recipients of some linear histories of the discipline inherited from the late 19th century and beginning of 20th century which they had been trained into reproducing but refrained from reflecting thereon and engaging therewith. By this account, the 'historical turn' witnessed a unprecedented challenge to the classical linear histories inherited from the late 19th century and the beginning of the 20th century by virtue of counter-histories,[14] greater critical or methodological scrutiny,[15] an embrace of the hermeneutic character of historical inquiries,[16] and eventually a rejection of the liberal concept of history inherited from the Enlightenment – that is history as both a scientific knowledge about the path and a route to truth.[17]

The foregoing has set the stage for the inquiry offered by this article. Taking for granted that international lawyers have historical self-awareness and are constantly historicizing, this article engages with the abovementioned 'historical turn' and thus international lawyers' recent and growing historiographical appetites. In particular, this article questions the critical attitude

13 Comp. Janne Nijman who has called it a turn to "history as theory". See Janne Nijman, 'Seeking Change by Doing History' (Amsterdam University Press, 2018) 9–10. Accessed 15th June 2018 at <https://ssrn.com/abstract=3167708>.

14 Koskenniemi, *Gentle Civilizer of Nations* (Cambridge University Press 2001); see D Kennedy, 'International Law and the Nineteenth Century: History of an Illusion' [1996] 17 QLR 99, 102–103.

15 This has been one of the main purpose of those works falling under the so-called 'Third World Approaches to International Law' (TWAIL).

16 See Keith Jenkins *On 'What is History'. From Carr and Elton to Rorty and White* (Roultledge 1995), 6: "History is one of a series of discourses about the world. These discourses do not create the world but they do appropriate it and give it all the meanings it has". On this aspect of the 'historical turn', see the remarks of J. Nijman Janne Nijman who has called it a turn to "history as theory". See Janne Nijman, 'Seeking Change by Doing History' (Amsterdam University Press, 2018) 9–10. Accessed 15th June 2018 at <https://ssrn.com/abstract=3167708>.

17 For some critical remarks on the idea of liberal conception of history, see Keith Jenkins, Re-thinking History (Routledge, 2003), 65 (he also holds that no one pressed the case so hard for history's scientificity as Marx). On the idea of postmodernism in history and historiography, see Beverley Southgate, 'Postmodernism' in Aviezer Tucker (ed), *A Companion to the Philosophy of History and Historiography* (Wiley-Blackwell 2011), 540. One of the leading postmodern historian is Hayden White, *Metahistory: The Historical Imagination in Nineteenth-century Europe* (John Hopkins University Press 1973). For a criticism of certaintist claims in history, see also Keith Jenkins, *On 'What is History'. From Carr and Elton to Rorty and White* (Roultledge 1995), esp 12–13. See also the work of E H H Carr who provided some critical groundwork for the subsequent rise of critical thinking in History. See E H H Carr, *What is History?* (2nd ed, CUP 1987) 15 (he argues that it is an heresy of the 19th century is to think that "history consists of the compilation of a maximum number of irrefutable and objective facts").

that is informing the critical histories that have been flourishing since the 'historical turn' in international law. This article makes the argument that the 'historical turn' falls short of being radically critical as the abounding critical histories which have come to populate the international literature over the last decades continue to be orchestrated along the very lines set by the linear historical narratives which they seek to question and disrupt. Said differently, this article makes the point that the critical histories that have accompanied the 'historical turn' have demonstrated a very limited critical attitude in that they have been complacent with the accepted markers, periodization and causal sequencing of the existing historical narratives about international law. This article will show the critical histories must move beyond a mere historiographical attitude that is confined to the markers, periodization and causal sequencing it seeks to displace or disrupt[18] and, promote radical historical critique. It will be demonstrated that to be critical, the historical turn can simply not be historiographical.

This claim about the limits of the critical attitude informing the critical histories that have been flourishing since the 'historical turn' in international law is articulated as follows. The article first spells out the understanding of historicization and history-writing it builds on, distinguishing between three key instruments in history-writing, namely markers, periodization and causal sequencing (1). Thereafter, the article sketches out the rise of linear disciplinary histories in international law at the end of the 19th century and the beginning of the 20th century, that is those disciplinary histories that later became the object of critical scrutiny after the so-called 'historical turn' (2). The attention then turns to the 'historical turn' and the upsurge of scholarly historiographical works as well as the proliferation of critical histories that seek to disrupt dominant linear disciplinary histories (3). The article then substantiates its main claim about the complacency of critical histories as they uphold the markers, periodization, and causal sequencing, of the mainstream linear disciplinary histories they seek to disrupt or displace (4). This leads the article to elaborate on the idea of the impossibility of critical historiography in international law and the necessity to move beyond a mere historiographical attitude with a view to embarking on radical historical critique understood here as an interventionist history-writing attitude that enables the production of new discourses about international law itself. (5). The concluding section returns to

---

18 In relation to deconstruction, Pierre Schlag argued that to avoid such a pitfall "deconstruction must start everywhere at once" (Pierre Schlag, '"Le Hors de Texte, C'est Moi" The Politics of Form and the Domestication of Deconstruction' [1990] 11 Cardozo Law Review 1631, 1648).

the idea of international law as a discipline and provides some epistemological remarks on the consequences of the radical critical attitude in history-writing promoted in this article (6).

Before developing this claim about the complacency of critical histories that have been flourishing since the 'historical turn' in international law, three important preliminary caveats are necessary. First, it must be made clear at the start that the story that unfolds in this article occasionally builds on some common linear disciplinary narratives. This is well illustrated by the articulation of the argument that follows around the so-called 'historical turn'. It could thus be critically scrutinized in the very same way as it evaluates recent critical histories. Second, the discussion that follows is restricted to a limited sample of historiographical works on international law, namely those found in Western Anglo-American scholarship. As a result, it does not prejudge anything about the state, the dynamics, and the possible limits of historiographical debates about international law in other parts of the world. Thirdly, and by the same token, it must be acknowledged that the charge against the Eurocentricism (or Westcentricism)[19] of contemporary critical histories in international law that accompanies the claim about the complacency of recent historiographical works is itself developed through the deployment of Eurocentric evaluative notions, Eurocentricism itself being one of them.

1 Markers, Periodization, Causal Sequencing, *effet du réel* and the Writing of Historical Narratives

The past is formless and has no meaning other than what is given to it in the present.[20] Said differently, the past lacks narrative form, order, and sequence, that, In that sense, it is the function of historical narratives to provide the formless past with meaning-giving form and to create what Barthes called

19 The word 'Eurocentricism' is used throughout the paper in a rather broad way as to include discourses and mode of thinking that are West-centric in general.

20 Hayden White 'The Question of Narrative in Contemporary Historical Theory' (1984) 23 (1) History and Theory 1, 26–57. See also Michael S Roth, 'Foreword: "All You've Got is History"' in Hayden White, *Metahistory. The Historical Imagination in the 19th-Century Europe* (JHU Press, 2014), xv and Beverley Southgate, 'Postmodernism' in Aviezer Tucker (ed), *A Companion to the Philosophy of History and Historiography* (Wiley-Blackwell, 2011), 540, 548. See contra P. Ricoeur, *'Time and Narative'* (Chicago University Press, 1983). For a criticism of this position, see Harold J. Berman, *Law and Revolution. The Formation of the Western Legal Tradition* (Harvard University Press, 1983), pp. 13–14.

the *effet du réel*[21] (reality effect[22]) in the present.[23] Narrativization, being about providing the formless pass with form, order, sequence and creating an *effet du réel* in the present,[24] is thus central in any historicizing exercise.[25]

For the sake of the argument made in the following sections, the role of narrativization in providing the formless and meaningless past with meaning-giving form must be unpacked further. The narrativization of the formless past is understood here as a complex operation that entails the organization of the past by virtue of some postulated units[26] which are then related to one another. More specifically, narrativizing the formless past necessitates the resort to some markers, periodization and causal sequencing. This narrativization of the past through markers, causal sequencing and periodization is a part of what Hayden White has called the act of "emplotment".[27] If this

---

21 Roland Barthes, 'le discours de l'histoire' (1967) 6 (4) Social Science Information 63, 74. The 'effet du rééľ' refers to the feeling that the form, order, and sequence of the past and the way in which the latter is narrated correspond to some kind of necessity.

22 This is how Alun Munslow translated effet réel of Barthes (xiv), see Alun Munslow, 'Preface' in Keith Jenkins, *On 'What is History'. From Carr and Elton to Rorty and White* (Roultledge 1995), xiv.

23 Beverley Southgate, 'Postmodernism', in Aviezer Tucker (ed), *A Companion to the Philosophy of History and Historiography* (Wiley-Blackwell 2011) 541. See also E H H Carr, *What is History?* (2nd ed, CUP 1987) 25 ("the historian belongs not to the past but to the present").

24 Comp with the definition of narrative of Michael S Roth, 'Foreword: "All You've Got is History"' in Hayden White, *Metahistory. The Historical Imagination in the 19th-Century Europe* (JHU Press, 2014), xv : "A narrative is a rhetorical strategy through which we mold our experience into a meaningful whole that can be communicated to others".

25 "One cannot historicize without narrativizing, because it is only by narrativization that a series of events can be transformed into a sequence, divided, into period, and represented as a process in which the substance of things can be said to change while their identities remain the same" Hayden White, 'Historical Discourse and Literary Writing' in Kuisma Korhonen (ed) *Tropes for the Past: Hayden White and the History/Literature Debate* (Rodopi 2006), 30. See Beverley Southgate, 'Postmodernism' in Aviezer Tucker (ed), *A Companion to the Philosophy of History and Historiography* (Wiley-Blackwell 2011), 548 ("the past itself lacks narrative form; order is not inherent in it, awaiting discovery, but is imposed upon it by historians; and in the construction of their narratives, historians are constrained by the linguistic and rhetorical usages of their own culture, 'emplotting' the pact in accordance with their own ideological positions").

26 Barthes, 'le discours de l'histoire' (1967) 6 (4) Social Science Information 63 69–70 (« L'énoncé historique doit se prêter à un découpage destiné à produire des unités du contenu, que l'on pourra ensuite classer »).

27 Hayden White, *Metahistory. The Historical Imagination in the 19th-Century Europe* (Johns Hopkins University Press 2014) 7 ("Providing the meaning of a story by identifying the kind of story that has been told is called explanation by emplotment"). See also Beverley Southgate, 'Postmodernism' in Aviezer Tucker (ed), *A Companion to the Philosophy of History and Historiography* (Wiley-Blackwell 2011) 548.

emplotment is successful, it will generate an *effet du réel*, thereby obfuscating the concrete choices in terms of markers, periodization, and causal sequencing and, ultimately the ideologies[28] and agendas[29] behind them.[30]

It is submitted here that the narrativization of the formless past and the creation of an *effet du réel* are organized around three key elements: markers, periodization, and causal sequencing. Narrativization provides a form and a meaning to the past by virtue of certain markers, periodization, and causal sequencing.[31] These various elements must be briefly unpacked here.

By *markers*, the article refers to those past texts, past actions, past events, past doctrines, past arguments, past theories, and past actors to which some relevance is given in the present and which are drawn on to build a historical narrative.[32] Marking the past means selecting and obliterating.[33] In the specific context of international legal discourses, these markers can be of very different types: the adoption of a landmark treaty or judicial decision, a factual or natural event, the publication of a specific scholarly work, the life of a certain author or political figure, etc. By virtue of narrativization, these markers are organized and ordered according to continuity and change (periodization) cause and effect (causal sequencing).[34] For instance, depending on periodization and causal sequencing, markers will be made watershed moments, turning points, points of rupture, caesura, crises, revolutionary moments, milestones, beginning and ends, transitional periods, etc.

---

28 Barthes, 'le discours de l'histoire' (1967) 6 (4) Social Science Information 63, 73; Keith Jenkins, *On 'What is History'. From Carr and Elton to Rorty and White* (Roultledge 1995), 20–22.

29 Ibid., 22 ("For some groups want a sanitized history where conflict and distress are absent; some want history to lead to quietism; some want history to embody rugged individualism, some to provide strategies and tactics for revolution, some to provide grounds for counter-revolution, and so on").

30 Barthes, 'le discours de l'histoire' (1967) 6 (4) Social Science Information 63, 71 « le discours 'objectif' … rejoint la situation du discours schizophrénique ; dans un cas comme dans l'autre, il y a censure radicale de l'énonciation » . See also Michael S Roth, 'Foreword: "All You've Got is History"' in Hayden White, *Metahistory. The Historical Imagination in the 19th-Century Europe* (JHU Press, 2014) xvi.

31 See the remarks of Beverley Southgate, 'Postmodernism', in Aviezer Tucker (ed), *A Companion to the Philosophy of History and Historiography* (Wiley-Blackwell 2011) 541.

32 E H H Carr, *What is History?* (2nd ed, CUP 1987) 11 ("Facts speak only when the historian calls on them: it is he who decides to which facts to give the floor, and in what order or context").

33 Ibid., 105.

34 Continuity and change as well as cause and effects are among what has been called the "couplets" of historical narratives. See Keith Jenkins, *On 'What is History'. From Carr and Elton to Rorty and White* (Roultledge 1995), 61.

Periodization is another key component of the narrativization that gives form to the formless past.[35] It boils down to the creation of temporal clusters[36] through an overemphasis of ruptures and discontinuities[37] that allows the organization of the formless past through beginning and ends.[38] Said differently, periodization is constituted by the setting of some chronological markers that provides a rhythm to the historical narrative concerned.[39] Periodization entails the cutting out of a great mass of materials that are made to embody a beginning or an end.[40] Periodization is often construed as a necessary component of any historical narrative because it performs important functions in the building of historical narratives.[41] For instance, periodization

35 Like causal sequencing, periodization is very modern and constitutes one of the legacies of the idea of history inherited from the Enlightenment. See Judith Surkis, 'When Was the Linguistic Turn? A Genealogy' (2012) 117 (3) American Historical Review 700, 701. The very idea of periodization has been the object of some intense discussion in History. Among general works on periodization, see R. Koselleck, *The Practice of Conceptual History* (Stanford University Press 2002); L L Besserman, *The Challenge of Periodization: Old Paradigms and New Perspectives* (Garland Publishing 1996); Marshall Brown, 'Periods and Resistance', (2001) 62 (4) Modern Language Quarterly 309; Jerry H. Bentley, 'Cross-Cultural Interaction and Periodization in World History' (1996) 101(3) American Historical Review 749; William A. Green, 'Periodizing World History' (1995 34 (2) History and Theory 99; P Stearns, 'Periodization in World History Teaching' (1987) 20 (4) History Teacher 561. For a powerful critique of Koselleck's model of periodization, see Kathleen Davis, *Periodization and Sovereignty: How Ideas of Feudalism and Secularization Govern the Politics of Time* (University of Philadelphia Press 2008).

36 William E Butler, 'Periodization and international law', in A Orakhelashvili (ed), *Research Handbook on the Theory and History of International Law* (Elgar 2011) 379.

37 Oliver Diggelman, 'The Periodization of the History of International Law' in Bardo Fassbender and Anne Peters (eds), *The Oxford Handbook of the History of International Law* (OUP, 2012) 996, 1003.

38 See the definition of William E Butler, 'Periodization and international law', in A Orakhelashvili (ed.), Research Handbook on the Theory and History of International Law (Elgar 2011), 379 ("Periodization may be understood as an analytical prism through which times past are organized into meaningful clusters in order to better understand the reasons for the occurrence of events or trends").

39 On the notion of periodization, see Oliver Diggelman, 'The Periodization of the History of International Law' in Bardo Fassbender and Anne Peters (eds), *The Oxford Handbook of the History of International Law* (OUP 2012).

40 Edward Said, *Orientalism* (Routledge 1978) 24 ("The idea of beginning, indeed the act of beginning, necessarily involves an act of delimitation by which something is cut out of a great mass of material, separated from the mass, and made to stand for, as well as be, a starting point, a beginning.")

41 See Reinhart Koselleck, 'On the Need for Theory in the Discipline of History' in Koselleck, *The Practice of Conceptual History*, 4. See also E H H Carr, *What is History?* (2nd ed, CUP 1987) 60; Oliver Diggelmann, 'The Periodization of the History of International Law' in Bardo Fassbender and Anne Peters (eds), *The Oxford Handbook of the History of*

comes with some spatio-temporal simplification and compression.[42] It allows moments of accelerations of the narration,[43] performs a pedagogical organization of the past[44] and makes the latter more accessible.[45] For the sake of the argument developed here, it is important to stress that periodization is an interpretive exercise.[46] Periods are not out there ready to be unearthed but are constituted.[47] This also means that the periodization at work in disciplinary histories about international law ought not follow the periodization offered by Historians.[48]

By *causal sequencing*, this article refers to the causal order that is constructed, in the present, between various markers and/or various periods.[49]

International Law (OUP, 2012) 996, 997. See also Wolfgang Preiser, 'History of International Law, Basic Questions and Principles' *Max Planck Encyclopedia of Public International Law* (2007) para 15 ("We accept that writers of the history of international law must also be allowed to apply the intellectual principle of order called categorization by period which is utilized by all historians, irrespective of specialization, when they perceive their task to be the comprehension retrospectively of an uninterrupted flow of events. It is regrettable that a living process should be thus divided into chronological and locational sections; yet, taking our limited powers of absorption into consideration, it cannot be avoided").

42 Judith Surkis, 'When Was the Linguistic Turn? A Genealogy' (2012) 117 (3) American Historical Review 700, 702.

43 Barthes, 'le discours de l'histoire' (1967) 6 (4) Social Science Information 63, at 67.

44 William E Butler, 'Periodization and International Law', in A Orakhelashvili (ed), *Research Handbook on the Theory and History of International Law* (Elgar 2011) 380.

45 Oliver Diggelman, 'The Periodization of the History of International Law' in Bardo Fassbender and Anne Peters (eds), *The Oxford Handbook of the History of International Law* (OUP, 2012) 996, 997.

46 Ibid., 1001. See also W E Butler, 'Some Reflections on the Periodization of Soviet Approaches to International law' in D D Barry, W E Butler, and G Ginsburgs (eds), *Contemporary Soviet Law: Essays in Honor of John N. Hazard* (Springer 1974), 213–225. See also William E Butler, 'Periodization and International Law', in A Orakhelashvili (ed), *Research Handbook on the Theory and History of International Law* (Elgar 2011) 380.

47 Diggelman, 'The Periodization of the History of International Law' in Bardo Fassbender and Anne Peters (eds), *The Oxford Handbook of the History of International Law* (OUP, 2012) 996, 999.

48 On the argument that historians of international law must develop their own periodizations and do not need to espouse those periodizations of histories of international relations, let alone general histories, see William E Butler, 'Periodization and International Law', in A Orakhelashvili (ed), *Research Handbook on the Theory and History of International Law* (Elgar 2011) 380, at 392.

49 See generally Hayden White, *Metahistory. The Historical Imagination in the 19th-Century Europe* (Johns Hopkins University Press, 2014) 275 (History-writing: naming, grouping, relating through causation that explain changes). See also the remarks on the various ways in which causalities and linearity are created, see Michel Foucault, *L'archéologie du savoir* (Gallimard, 1969), pp. 18–19 and p. 84.

In fact, crude chronicles of facts cannot constitute a historical narrative.[50] Organizing markers and periods in an orderly sequence of cause and effects is central in narrativizing.[51] Causal sequencing is thus dependent on prior marking and periodization. There are a multitude of ways in which markers and periods can be organized in an orderly sequence of cause and effects. Among many others, progress narrative is one way to articulate markers and periods. The finding of cyclical patterns is another.[52] The same holds for the findings of development, evolution and influence.[53] Such causality is the result of an interpretive exercise too and is informed by value judgment, ideology, agendas, etc.[54]

According to the perspective adopted here and especially the abovementioned understanding of markers, periodization, and causal sequencing, it should be clear by now that, for the sake of the argument made in this article, what produces a valid historical narrative – and thus a valid emplotment – is not its correspondence with facts. Historical facts are part of the very form and meaning that are given to the past. They are the products of the *effet du réel* produced through an emplotment, that is a set of choices in terms of markers, causal sequence and periodization. This also means that no specific assemblage of markers, periodization and causal sequencing can possibly secure consensus or correspond to any empirical truth. Empirical truth about the past is no longer an option, the question becoming a matter of choice between contending narratives, and hence between markers, periodization, and causal sequencing.[55] The perspective adopted thus points to the impossibility of determining one single given and unique method to determine the meaning of the past and thus the impossibility to generate one single universal grand historical narrative about international law.[56] Indeed, there are a huge variety of possible assemblages of markers, periodizations, and causal

---

50 Barthes, 'le discours de l'histoire' (1967) 6 (4) Social Science Information 63, 72. See also Jenkins, *On 'What is History'. From Carr and Elton to Rorty and White* (Roultledge 1995), 40

51 E H H Carr, *What is History?* (2nd ed, CUP 1987)88 (who argues that creating orderly sequence is part of History since the Enlightenment).

52 Diggelman, 'The Periodization of the History of International Law' in Bardo Fassbender and Anne Peters (eds), *The Oxford Handbook of the History of International Law* (OUP, 2012) 996, 1007.

53 Michel Foucault, *L'archéologie du savoir* (Gallimard, 1969), pp. 33–34.

54 E H H Carr, *What is History?* (2nd ed, CUP 1987) 103, 107. Michel Foucault, *L'archéologie du savoir* (Gallimard, 1969), at 34–35; Hans-Georg Gadamer, *Truth and Method*, Bloomsbury, 2013, at xxiii.

55 See the remarks of Beverley Southgate, 'Postmodernism' in Aviezer Tucker (ed) *A Companion to the Philosophy of History and Historiography* (Wiley-Blackwell 2011) 541.

56 Jenkins, *On 'What is History'. From Carr and Elton to Rorty and White* (Roultledge 1995), 40.

sequencing available to international lawyers.[57] The number of past events, texts, scholarly works, figures which can be elevated into markers and the way in which they are causally arranged and periodized in order to generate an *effet du réel* can be multiplied indefinitely. In other words, the range of possible historical narratives that international lawyers can choose to generate is immense.[58]

The availability of such a multitude of markers, periodizations, and causal sequencing – and thus of historical narratives – bears important epistemological consequences. In fact, in the absence of any dominant historical narrative, battles of markers, periodization and causal sequencing are bound to rage, historical narratives, counter-narratives, and counter-counter-narratives being constantly struck at one another. As was just said, such battles abate only as some historical narratives, and thus certain assemblages of markers, periodization, and causal sequencing secure dominance through greater social acceptance.[59] Actually, a historical narrative is deemed valid because it rests on markers, a periodization and causal sequencing that are socially accepted.[60]

Against the backdrop of the conceptual framework that has just been presented, the argument made in this article can now be more precisely and rigorously rephrased. It has been said that, after the 'historical turn', many international lawyers have paid greater attention to the historical narratives at work in international legal thought and practice while making the evaluation of such narratives a significant part of their scholarly works. This has led, it has been argued, to an upsurge in historiographical works in international legal scholarship. This article argues that the abounding 'critical' histories that have flourished over the last decades, although aiming at disrupting the *effet de réel* of common linear disciplinary histories, have remained imprisoned in the very emplotment of the latter. In particular, this article makes the point that most

---

57 It is one of the greatest merit of Hayden Wide to have offered us a taxonomy of the emplotments techniques of 19th century historians. He distinguishes four modes of articulation by which the historian can gain explanatory effect of a specific kind as well as 4 emplotment. See Hayden White, *Metahistory. The Historical Imagination in the 19th-Century Europe* (Johns Hopkins University Press, 2014), 1–41. For a discussion of various ways to treat and organize historical materials see also Jenkins, *On 'What is History'. From Carr and Elton to Rorty and White* (Roultledge 1995), 25–28.

58 In the same sense, Matthew Craven, 'Introduction: International Law and Its Histories' in Matthew Craven, Malgosia Fitzmaurice and Maria Vogiatzi (eds), *Time, History and International Law* (Brill 2007) 3.

59 For a rejection of relativism and the idea that any interpretation is good as another, see E H H Carr, *What is History?* (2nd ed, CUP 1987) 27.

60 Hayden White, *Metahistory. The Historical Imagination in the 19th-Century Europe* (Johns Hopkins University Press, 2014), 79.

critical histories found in the international legal scholarship are articulated around the very same markers, periodization and causal sequencing through which earlier dominant linear disciplinary histories had been organized and by virtue of which they were producing their *effet du réel*. Contemporary critical histories, it is argued, uphold, rather than disrupt, the markers, periodization and causal sequencing of linear histories they take issue with.

2 The Rise of Disciplinary Histories in International Law

Before elucidating and illustrating the 'historical turn' and its alleged manifestations, a few considerations must be formulated on the very disciplinary histories which the critical histories have been seeking to disrupt and displace. In this regard, it must preliminarily be highlighted that the systematic creation of disciplinary histories in international law is a rather recent phenomenon.[61] The first comprehensive linear histories of international law is usually associated with the professionalization of the discipline outside diplomatic circles[62] and the rise of international law as an academic discipline in the second half of the 19th century and the beginning of the 20th century.[63]

61 For an exception, see Robert Plumer Ward, *An Enquiry into the Foundation and History of the Law of Nations, from the Time of the Greeks and Romans to the Age of Grotius* (Strahan and Woodfall, 1795). Walter Rech has argued that Ward's account vindicated a very relativist claim about international law and the idea of all nations abiding by the same rules while advocating regionalist understanding of the law of nations with a view to isolating France (see the discussion in Walter Rech, 'International Law, Empire, and the Relative Indeterminacy of Narrative' in Martti Koskenniemi, Walter Rech, and Manuel Jimenez Fonseca (eds), *International Law and Empire* (OUP 2017) 70–73. On Ward, see also the remarks of Wolfgang Preiser, 'History of International Law, Basic Questions and Principles' *Max Planck Encyclopedia of Public International Law* (2007) para 1.

62 Most famous of them are Hugo Grotius and Friedrich Fromhold von Martens. On Hugo Grotius, see J Haskell, 'Hugo Grotius in the Contemporary Memory of International Law: Secularism, Liberalism, and the Politics of Restatement and Denial' in J M Beneyto, D Kennedy, J Corti Varela and J Haskell (eds.) *New approaches to international law: the European and the American experiences* (Asser Press 2012) 123–150. On Martens, see M Koskenniemi, 'Into Positivism: Georg Friedrich von Martens (1756–1821) and Modern International Law' [2008] 15 *Constellations* 189.

63 Martti Koskenniemi, 'A History of International Law Histories' in Bardo Fassbender and Anne Peters, *The Oxford Handbook of International Law* (OUP 2012) 943; Martti Koskenniemi, 'Histories of International Law: Significance and Problems for a Critical View' (2013) 27 Temple International and Comparative Law Journal 215, 220. On self-consciousness of these international lawyers, see Matthew Craven, 'The Invention of a Tradition: Westlake, The Berlin Conference and the Historicisation of International Law'

Indeed, it is with international law becoming a self-standing object of studies in university institutions which created professorships specifically dedicated to the teaching of international law[64] as well as the primary focus of learned

---

in Luigi Nuzzo and Miloš Vec, *Constructing International Law: The Birth of a Discipline* (Klostermann 2012) 37. See also Benjamin Allen Coates, *Legalist Empire. International Law and American Foreign Relations in the Early Twentieth Century* (OUP, 2016) 18–19.

64 Stephen C Neff reports that an early professorship in the subject was established at the University of Turin in 1851. The Chichele Chair of International Law and Diplomacy was established in 1859 at Oxford University. The Whewell Chair in International Law at Cambridge University was created in 1867. Although it had tried to appoint Wheaton in the 1840s, Harvard Law School appointed its first international law professors in 1898. See Stephen C Neff, *Justice Among Nations* (Harvard University Press 2014) 304. See also M Koskenniemi, 'Nationalism, Universalism, Empire: International Law in 1871 and 1919', talk delivered at Columbia University (Newyork April 2005) available at www.helsinki.fi/eci/Publications/talks_papers_MK.html (last accessed 4 Dec. 2015); See also the remarks of I de la Rasilia del Moral, 'The Ambivalent Shadow of the Pre-Wilsonian Rise of International Law' [2014] 7 ELR 2 (he argues that in the wake of the independence of the American Republics from Spain, the university teaching of international law emerged comparatively earlier in the US than in Europe, maybe with the exception of Spain. The first courses of international law in the United States were taught in 1846 at Yale by Theodore Woolsey and Francis Lieber later on). For some general remarks on the professionalization of international law see J. d'Aspremont, The professionalization of international law in J d'Aspremont and others, *International Law as Profession* (CUP 2017); Anne Orford, 'Scientific Reason and the Discipline of International Law' [2014] 25 European Journal of International Law 369, 373; Benjamin Allen Coates, *Legalist Empire. International Law and American Foreign Relations in the Early Twentieth Century* (OUP, 2016) 18–21, 61–68. It must be emphasized that notwithstanding the systemic production of publications and the inclusion in the curriculum of law schools, it took a few more decades to witness the rise of a cohort of professionals whose training and practice were entirely and exclusively in the field of international law. In fact, at the beginning of the 20th century, international law was rarely a career in itself and many of the influential figures of the time came late to the field. It suffices to remember the profile of the first generation of judges of the Permanent Court of International Justice. Obviously the recruitment of these first 'professionals' did not prove easy as there was not an existing cohort of ready-trained international lawyers; many of the first professionals of international law were drawn from other circles, especially private international law. Probably with the exception of scholarship and teaching, it took another decade for the emergence of a group of professionals devoted to the practice of international law. In some specific areas, such as trade law, it took even longer to witness the consolidation of a generation of professionals trained as international lawyers. For some general remarks, see A Mills, 'The Private History of International Law' [2006] 55 ICLQ 1–50. O. Spiermann, *International Legal Argument in the Permanent Court of International Justice: The Rise of the International Judiciary* (Cambridge University Press 2005).

societies and scholarly periodicals[65] that the perceived need to endow the field with a disciplinary history became very pressing.[66] For international lawyers of the time, providing a disciplinary history to international law[67] proved a conscious way to confirm the maturity and respectability,[68] identity,[69] and scientificity[70] of the field, entrench it in a tradition[71] and make it a universal necessity.[72] It is in this context that the first systematic and comprehensive studies about the 'history' of international law came to be produced. The work

65 See eg the creation of the *Revue Générale de Droit International et de Legislation Comparée* and later the *Revue Générale de Droit International Public* in 1894. See generally S Neff, *Justice Among Nations: A History of International Law* (Harvard University Press 2014) 300.

66 For a famous manifestation of this feeling of a need for a disciplinary history, see L Oppenheim, 'The Science of International Law: Its Task and Method' (1908) 2 (2) American Journal of International Law 313. He wrote: "History of international law is certainly the most neglected province of it" and added "The master-historian of international law has still to come" (p. 316). For a discussion of Oppenheim's claim, see Amanda Perreau-Saussine, 'A Case Study on Jurisprudence as a Source of International Law: Oppenheim's Influence' in Matthew Craven, Malgosia Fitzmaurice and Maria Vogiatzi (eds), *Time, History and International Law* (Brill 2007) 100; see also Monica Garcia-Salmones Rovira, *The Project of Positivism in International Law* (OUP 2013).

67 Matthew Craven, 'The Invention of a Tradition: Westlake, The Berlin Conference and the Historicisation of International Law' in Luigi Nuzzo and Miloš Vec, *Constructing International Law: The Birth of a Discipline* (Klostermann 2012) 36. Describing this historical self-consciousness is one of the main purpose of Koskenniemi's *The Gentle Civilizer of Nations: The Rise and Fall of International Law 1870–1960* (Cambridge University Press 2001).

68 Liliana Obregon, 'Writing International Legal History: An Overview', 7 Monde(s), (2015) 95, at 110 (she argues that this was the avowed goal of Nys).

69 Thomas Kleinlein, 'International Legal Thought: Creation of a Tradition and the Potential of Disciplinary Self-Reflection' in Giuliana Ziccardi Capaldo, *The Global Community: Yearbook of International Law and Jurisprudence 2016* (OUP 2016) 811, 812.

70 For some critical remarks, see Anne Orford, 'Scientific Reason and the Discipline of International Law' [2014] 25 European Journal of International Law 369. See also Luigi Nuzzo, "The Birth of an Imperial Location: Comparative Perspectives on Western Colonialism in China" 31 Leiden Journal of International Law (2018) 569, at 596.

71 Thomas Kleinlein, 'International Legal Thought: Creation of a Tradition and the Potential of Disciplinary Self-Reflection' in Giuliana Ziccardi Capaldo, *The Global Community: Yearbook of International Law and Jurisprudence 2016* (OUP 2016) 811, at 816. See also Anne Orford, 'International Law and the Limits of History' in W Werner and others (eds), *The Law of International Lawyers: Reading Martti Koskenniemi* (CUP 2015) 307 (On the notion of invention of tradition, see Eric Hobsbawm, 'Introduction: inventing traditions' in E Hobsbawm and T Ranger (eds), *The Invention of Tradition* (Cambridge University Press 1983) 1–14.

72 BS Chimini, 'The Past, Present, and Future of International Law: A Critical Third World Approach' 8 Melbourne Journal of International Law 499–516, at 502.

of Wheaton,[73] Laurent,[74] and Nys[75] quickly acquired some referential status in this respect.[76] In the United States, James Brown Scott[77] also invested a lot in providing the field with a disciplinary history, albeit a slightly different variant of that prevalent in Europe at the time.[78]

---

73 Henry Wheaton worked extensively on the history of the law of nations and produced Histoire des Progrès du Droit des Gens en Europe et en Amérique Depuis la Paix de Westphalie jusqu'à nos Jours (Leipzig, Brockhaus, 1841), later translated as *A History of the Law of Nations in Europe and America from the Earliest Times to the Treaty of Washington* (New York; Gould, Banks & Co.; 1845). On the ambitions behind Wheaton's writing of a history of international law see Liliana Obregon, 'Writing International Legal History: An Overview', 7 Monde(s), (2015) 95, at 103–105.

74 François Laurent, *Histoires du droit des gens et des relations internationales* (Lelong, 18 volumes). On the context in which Laurent embarked on the writing of his colossal work, see Liliana Obregon, 'Writing International Legal History: An Overview', 7 Monde(s), (2015) 95, at 105–106.

75 Ernest Nys, *Les origines du droit international* (Castaigne, 1894). On the very rich work of Ernest Nys, see Henri Rolin, « Notice sur Ernest Nys », Revue de l'Université de Bruxelles, t. IV, 1951–1952, pp. 349–357 ; see also Jean Salmon, « notice Ernest Nys », Nouvelle biographie nationale, tome 9, Académie royale de Belgique, 2007, pp. 283–285. Nys is said to have been one of the first to put the emphasis on Vitoria's writing and elevate him into a founding father of the discipline. See Liliana Obregon, 'Writing International Legal History: An Overview', 7 Monde(s), (2015) 95, at 110.

76 Other historical works must also be mentioned albeit they have been less influential. See e.g. A Pillet (ed), *Les Fondateurs du Droit International* (Giard et Brière, 1904). See also the historical works mentioned by D. Armitage and J. Pitts, " 'This Modern Grotius': An Introduction to the Life and Thought of C.H. Alexandrowicz", in C. H. Alexandrowicz, *The Law of Nations in Global History* (OUP, 2017), p. 2.

77 On James Brown Scott's efforts to build a history for the discipline, see the remarks Benjamin Allen Coates, *Legalist Empire. International Law and American Foreign Relations in the Early Twentieth Century* (OUP, 2016) 68–71.

78 It is well-known that Scott took a dim look at the status of Grotius in the dominant European disciplinary histories and sought to put the emphasis on Grotius predecessors. He did so by publishing and editing several volumes of the series "Classics of International Law" between 1911 and 1950. For some critical remarks on the disciplinary history vindicated by Scott and his emphasis on Vitoria, Suarez, Baltasar de Ayala, Alberico Gentili see José-Manuel Barreto, 'Cerberus: Rethinking Grotius and the Westphalian System' in Martti Koskenniemi, Walter Rech, and Manuel Jimenez Fonseca (eds), *International Law and Empire* (OUP, 2017) 149, 153; Thomas Kleinlein, 'International Legal Thought: Creation of a Tradition and the Potential of Disciplinary Self-Reflection' in Giuliana Ziccardi Capaldo, *The Global Community: Yearbook of International Law and Jurisprudence 2016* (OUP 2016) 811, 816; Stephen Neff, *Justice Among Nations. A History of International Law* (Harvard University Press, 2014) 381; Randall Lesaffer, 'The classical law of nations (1500–1800)' in A Orakhelashvili (ed), *Research Handbook on the Theory and History of International Law* (Elgar 2011) 410. The emphasis of Scott on Vitoria by Scott famously led Anthonie Anghie to show how the violence in Vitoria played in American legal thought (see Anthony Anghie 'Francisco De Vitoria and the Colonial Origins of International Law'

Unsurprisingly, when embarking on the creation of a disciplinary history, those 19th and 20th centuries international lawyers came to choose specific markers, periodization, and causal sequencing, demonstrating on that occasion some remarkable historical self-consciousness.[79] For instance, as far as international law's origin is concerned, a huge variety markers were available to mark the beginning of the discipline. As is well-known, the Peace of Westphalia was picked and, by virtue of a new periodization and causal sequencing, was made a foundational event for the field.[80] It is true that there has been some debate as to who exactly came to elevate Westphalia in the linchpin of the causal sequencing and periodization of the linear disciplinary histories of international law.[81] It remains that the choice for Westphalia as a central marker and the whole imaginary associated with these two modest bilateral treaties[82] allowed the beginning of international law not only to

[1996] 5 Social and Legal Studies 321; Antony Anghie, *Imperialism, Sovereignty and the Making of International Law* (Cambridge: Cambridge University Press 2004) 14). See the remarks of Anne Orford n (3).

79 For instance, there seems to be no doubt that Lauterpacht wrote the 'Grotian Tradition' with an acute historical self-consciousness and the ambition of writing disciplinary history. Martti Koskenniemi writes: "Lauterpacht's oeuvre and career constitute a striking illustration of an international legal consciousness that sought to resuscitate the rationalism of the nineteenth century in the aftermath of the First World War but used up its emancipatory potential in the doctrinal struggles of the 1930s" (Martti Konskenniemi, 'Lauterpacht : The Victorian Tradition in International Law' 8 (2) EJIL 215, 261). In the same sense, see Oona A Hathaway and Scott J Shapiro, *The Internationalists. How a Radical Plan to Outlaw War Remade the World* (Simon & Schuster 2017) 300.

80 On the arbitrariness of the choice for 1648, see Matthew Craven, 'Introduction: International Law and Its Histories' in Matthew Craven, Malgosia Fitzmaurice and Maria Vogiatzi (eds), *Time, History and International Law* (Brill 2007), at 8. See also Bardo Fassbender, 'Peace of Westphalia (1648)' *Max Planck Encyclopedia of Public International Law* (2011) para. 7, 18–19.

81 For his part Andreas Osiander has located it in the work of Nys. (See A Osiander, 'Sovereignty, 'International Relations, and the Westphalian Myth' (2001) 55 (2) International Organization 251). For José-Manuel Barreto the origin of this periodization goes back as early as 1845 with Henry Wheaton. (see José-Manuel Barreto, , 'Cerberus: Rethinking Grotius and the Westphalian System' in Martti Koskenniemi, Walter Rech, and Manuel Jimenez Fonseca (eds), *International Law and Empire* (OUP, 2017) 159–160). For the claim that the myth of Westphalia was created by Leo Gross in the middle of the 20th century, see Luis Eslava, Michael Fakhri, and Vasuki Nesiah, Bandung, *Global History and International Law. Critical Pasts and Pending Futures* (CUP 2017) 15 (referring to Leo Gross, 'The Peace of Westphalia, 1648–1948'[1948] 42 American Journal of International Law 29). See also the remarks of Jennifer Pitts, 'Empire and Legal Universalism in the Eighteenth Century' (2012) 117 (1) American Historical Review 92, 93.

82 See A Osiander, 'Sovereignty, International Relations, and the Westphalian Myth' (2001) 55 (2) International Organization 251.

be associated with modernity but was also to be located in Europe,[83] thereby making the history of international law a part of the history of Western civilization and vice-versa.[84]

The above efforts devoted to the writing of new linear disciplinary histories also entailed the – conscious –[85] picking of some founding fathers and heroes.[86]

83 On the idea that 1648 makes the history of international law so European and Northern and pushes to the margins of the experience of African, Asian, or South American societies, see Matthew Craven, 'Introduction: International Law and Its Histories' in Matthew Craven, Malgosia Fitzmaurice and Maria Vogiatzi (eds), *Time, History and International Law* (Brill 2007) at 8.

84 For an illustration of the claim that history of international law is a branch of the history of Western civilization, see L Oppenheim, 'The Science of International Law: Its Task and Method' (1908) 2 (2) American Journal of International Law 313, 317.

85 It is noteworthy to note that Lauterpacht – traditionally seen as one of the architects of Grotius towering posture – recognizes his own recuperation of Grotius work. See Hersch Lauterpacht, 'The Grotian Tradition in International Law' [1946] 23 The British Yearbook of International Law 1, 5 ("We cannot even consider him as what is usually described as a 'Grotian' who has accomplished a workable synthesis of natural law and state practice. The fact seems to be that on most subjects which he discusses in his treatise it is impossible to say what is Grotius's view of the legal position"). See also ibid., 17: "If it is inaccurate to say that Grotius is the founder of modern international law, it is equally true that the necessity for an international law secured to the work of Grotius a place which otherwise it might not have acquired". See also ibid., 51: "Grotius did not create international law. Law is not made by writers. What Grotius did was to endow international law with unprecedented dignity and authority by making it part not only of a general system of jurisprudence but also of a universal moral code". Interestingly, despite showing some great historical self-consciousness, Lauterpacht denies that the canonization of Grotius is his. Instead, the canonization of Grotius by Lauterpacht is conducted empirically, that is by reference to the invocation of its work in scholarship and practice. Lauterpacht claims that Grotius's positions have become an "integral part of the doctrine and of the practice of the modern law of nations" (ibid., 22). See also ibid., 52: "De Jure Belli ac Pacis is pre-eminently a treatise which must be judged not by reference to its method, but by its influence on the doctrine and on the practice of the law of nations". This self-consciousness of Grotius led Martti Koskenniemi to write the following about Grotius: "To find a place for law in a dangerous time, Lauterpacht looks back into the middle of the nineteenth century and hopes to resuscitate its liberal rationalism and its ideal of the rule of law, its belief in progress, its certainty about the sense and direction of history …" (Koskenniemi *Gentle Civilizer of Nations* (Cambridge University Press 2001, 355).

86 On the reasons why Grotius was elected the father of international law in the context of the professionalization of the discipline, see Benjamin Allen Coates (n 71) 18. For Alain Wijffels, the success of Gentili and Grotius can be explained because their work could be read as "general handbooks of the law of nations in the modern sense", thereby making international law a specialized branch of the law in its own right They were the first authors to deal comprehensively with the law of nations. See Alain Wijffels, 'Early-modern scholarship on international law' in A Orakhelashvili (ed), *Research Handbook on the Theory and History of International Law* (Elgar 2011) 23, 42–44.

Although he had been cited in 17th and 18th centuries works,[87] Grotius, for a variety of reasons,[88] came to be elevated into one of the architects of the discipline by the authors of disciplinary histories in the end of the 19th century and the beginning of the 20th century. It is true that, until today, there still has been some debate – just like for the paternity of the marker of Westphalia – as to who in the 20th century actually proved the most instrumental in the elevation of Grotius into a towering figure of these new disciplinary histories.[89] Yet, there generally is a consensus that it is the 20th century that made Grotius a

87 See Lauterpacht discussing the references to Grotius by Pufendorf, Bynkershoek, Wolff, and Vattel (Hersch Lauterpacht, 'The Grotian Tradition in International Law' [1946] 23 The British Yearbook of International Law 1, 15–16).

88 Various explanations have been provided as to why Grotius was preferred to other writers. See eg Martti Koskenniemi who has referred to his "naturalist, scientifically-orientated way to look at the universe" as being instrumental in his success in the 19th and 20th century. See Martti Koskenniemi, 'Histories of International Law: Significance and Problems for a Critical View' [2013] 27 Temple International and Comparative Law Journal 215, 217. Michael Lobban has argued that making Grotius and Vattel a central marker was a way to respond to the attack of Austin against international law. Michael Lobban, 'English Approaches to International Law in the Nineteenth Century' in Matthew Craven, Malgosia Fitzmaurice and Maria Vogiatzi (eds), *Time, History and International Law* (Brill 2007) 80. It is noteworthy that, in 1946, Lauterpacht already thought to explain the external and internal contingency that were conducive to the elevation of Lauterpacht in a towering figure. See Hersch Lauterpacht, Hersch Lauterpacht, 'The Grotian Tradition in International Law' [1946] 23 The British Yearbook of International Law 1, 18–19. See also J Haskell, 'Hugo Grotius in the Contemporary Memory of International Law: Secularism, Liberalism, and the Politics of Restatement and Denial' in J M Beneyto, D Kennedy, J Corti Varela and J Haskell (eds), *New approaches to international law: the European and the American experiences* (Asser Press 2012) 123–150.

89 Whilst it is commonly acknowledged that Hersch Lauterpacht's famous *The Grotian Tradition of International Law* decisively confirmed to "fatherhood" of Grotius in the disciplinary history of international law (See Hersch Lauterpacht, 'The Grotian Tradition in International Law' [1946] 23 The British Yearbook of International Law 1), Randall Lesaffer has argued that, before being famously popularized by Hersch Lauterpacht, "(t)he recuperation of the thought of the Dutch humanist Hugo Grotius (1583–1645), as a precursor to an international society in which the license of the sovereign State is limited through law, reaches back as far as Cornelis van Vollenhoven's *The Three States in the Evolution of the Law of Nations*, first published in 1918 (Randall Lesaffer, 'The Grotian Tradition Revisited: Change and Continuity in the History of International Law' (2003) 73 (1) British Yearbook of International Law (2002) 103, 108 (referring to Cornelis van Vollenhover, De drie treden van het volkenrecht (The Hague, 1918))). Lesaffer also mentions Maurice Bourquin as one of the author of such recuperation (ibid., 108), citing Maurice Bourquin, Grotius et les tendances actuelles du droit international' [1926] 7 Revue de Droit International et de Legislation Comparée 85, 86. Oppenheim claimed that Grotius is the father of international law also he did not create the law of nations (L Oppenheim, 'The Science of

key marker of the disciplinary history of international law and *De Jure Belli ac Paci* one of the canonical texts of international legal thought.[90]

Choices of markers, periodization, and causal sequencing are, as was discussed in the previous section, informed by certain agendas and ideologies. Inevitably, the linear disciplinary histories with which international law was endowed and the abovementioned choices in terms of markers, periodization, and causal sequencing came with all sorts of presuppositions as to the role of international law, what it is meant to achieve, which actors should have a say and which place they should occupy, and more generally, the identity of the discipline itself and its shared ethos.[91] One of the most common presuppositions pervading such linear disciplinary histories probably lies in the search for universal principles and institutions[92] in a way that consolidated international

---

International Law: Its Task and Method' (1908) 2 (2) American Journal of International Law 313, 328).

90 There are a few exceptions. José-Manuel Barreto, while giving Nys a central role in the elevation of Grotius into the father of international law, has argued that the idea of Grotius as the father of modern international law is quite old. Argues that already in the early 18th century, Gianbattista Vico called Grotius the jurist of the human race. José-Manuel Barreto, 'Cerberus: Rethinking Grotius and the Westphalian System' in Martti Koskenniemi, Walter Rech, and Manuel Jimenez Fonseca (eds), *International Law and Empire* (OUP, 2017) 152–154. Anne Orford has argued that Whewell published in 1853 a new edition of De Juri Belli et Pacis Libri Tres and in the preface he praised the scheme of reasoning of Grotius and its reliance upon solid philosophical principles constantly applied (See Anne Orford, 'Scientific Reason and the Discipline of International Law' [2014] 25 European Journal of International Law 369, 374)

91 Matthew Craven, 'Introduction: International Law and Its Histories' in Matthew Craven, Malgosia Fitzmaurice and Maria Vogiatzi (eds), *Time, History and International Law* (Brill 2007), at 8 ("To write a history (or more emphatically the history) of international law necessarily involves, in other words, setting out in advance the parameters of the discipline (in terms of its subjects and sources, its actors and modes of engagement) and the narration of a story in which the identity of the discipline itself is held relatively constant and in which varied and opposing voices are, for purposes of the narrative itself, silenced or pushed to one side").

92 Martti Koskenniemi, 'A History of International Law Histories' in Bardo Fassbender and Anne Peters, *The Oxford Handbook of International Law* (OUP 2012), 945; See also Anne Orford, 'Scientific Reason and the Discipline of International Law' [2014] 25 European Journal of International Law 369.

law as one of the main "received narratives of modernist progress"[93] and its status as a scientific discipline.[94]

Interestingly those linear disciplinary histories produced in the late 19th and beginning of the 20th century, remained at work most of the 20th century without undergoing any serious challenge or disruption.[95] It is true that the markers, periodization and causal sequencing of those histories were occasionally nuanced,[96] for instance by expending the roots of modern

93 For an expression of the faith in the progress of international law, see L Oppenheim, 'The Science of International Law: Its Task and Method' (1908) 2 (2) American Journal of International Law 313, 317 (on p. 317, he speaks of the "victory of international law over international anarchy"). For some critical remarks on international law as the recipient of a progressive narrative, see Martti Koskenniemi, 'Histories of International Law: Significance and Problems for a Critical View' [2013] 27 Temple International and Comparative Law Journal 215, 217.

94 For an illustration of the feeling that disciplinary history contributes to the scientificity of the field, see L Oppenheim, 'The Science of International Law: Its Task and Method' (1908) 2 (2) American Journal of International Law 313, 315–317. For some critical remarks on how history contributed to the feeling of scientificity, see Anne Orford, 'Scientific Reason and the Discipline of International Law' [2014] 25 European Journal of International Law 369, 370. On the compatibility between scientific view and progress narrative, see Hayden White, *Metahistory. The Historical Imagination in the 19th-Century Europe* (Johns Hopkins University Press, 2014), 47–48.

95 See e.g. H. Lauterpacht, *Oppenheim's International Law* (Longman, 1955, 8th edition), 72–88; Charles de Visscher, Théories et Réalités en Droit International Public (4th ed., Pedone, 1970), 11–86. See also P. Guggenheim, "Les Origines de la Notion autonome du Droit des Gens", in Symbolae Verzijl (Nijhoff, 1958), pp. 177–189. On the persistence of these histories, see also Anthony Carty, "Interwar German Theories of International Law: The Psychoanalytical and Phenomenological Perspectives of Hans Kelsen and Carl Schmitt" 16 Cardozo Law Review 1235 p. 1235); J.-L. Brierly, The Law of Nations. An Introduction to the International Law of Peace (6th ed. Clarendon Press, 1963), 1–40. On the persistence of these histories, see also Anthony Carty, 'Interwar German Theories of International Law: The Psychoanalytical and Phenomenological Perspectives of Hans Kelsen and Carl Schmitt' (1995) 16 (2) Cardozo Law Review 1235.

96 For another variant of such linear histories, see See eg Onuma Yasuaki, *International Law in a Transcivilizational World* (CUP 2017) 11–20. See also Oona A. Hathaway and Scott J. Shapiro, *The Internationalists. How a Radical Plan to Outlaw War Remade the World* (Simon & Schuster 2017). For another nuance to the common periodization and causal sequencing, see eg Wilhelm Grewe, *The epochs of international law*; (Michael Byers trs, de Gruyter 2000). For criticisms of Grewe's realistic view of law as a superstructural offshoot of projects and activities expanding from the imperial center to its peripheries as well as for its overly simple view of what power is and how it works, see Martti Koskenniemi, 'Histories of International Law: Significance and Problems for a Critical View' [2013] 27 Temple International and Comparative Law Journal 215, 219). See also Martti Koskenniemi, 'A History of International Law Histories' in Bardo Fassbender and Anne Peters, *The Oxford Handbook of International Law* (OUP 2012) 962.

international law in the Antiquity.[97] Yet, that did not fundamentally alter the overall configuration and composition of the linear disciplinary narratives designed in the late 19th and beginning of the 20th century. This resilience, however, must be qualified in one specific respect. There is one aspect of these linear disciplinary histories that came to be subject to a severe alteration in the first half of the 20th century. It is the growing feeling of exceptionalism[98] experienced by 20th century international lawyers, and especially by inter-war international lawyers,[99] which led the latter to distance themselves from one dimension of the linear historical narratives inherited from the late 19th century international lawyers. In fact, with a view to vindicating the felt uniqueness of their time,[100] 20th century international lawyers, and especially the academics of the interbellum,[101] amended the common causal sequencing

97 On the traditional tracing back of international law to Antiquity in 20th century's work, See Alexander Orakhelashvili, 'The relevance of theory and history – the essence and origins of international law' in A Orakhelashvili (ed), *Research Handbook on the Theory and History of International Law* (Elgar 2011) 19–22. See also David J. Bederman, *International Law in Antiquity* (CUP 2004) (he does not claim that modern international law should traced back to antiquity but seeks to rehabilitate the ancient law of nations and respond to the detractors of an ancient laws of nations). For some methodological remarks on the construction of international law in Antiquity, see -Slim Laghmani, "Les Origines du droit international public et le concept de discours fondateur", in in P.-M. Dupuy and V. Chetail (eds), *The Roots of International Law. Liber Amicorum Peter Haggenmacher* (Nijhoff, 2014), 449–464.

98 Kennedy writes: "For today's international lawyer, the twentieth century is truly an exceptional one, a time of new ideas, new institutions, new scholarly methods, and new roles for international lawyers and scholars. More than a gap in memory, the nineteenth century offers an image of the premodern, a baseline against which to measure the discipline's progress and this century's exceptionalism" (D Kennedy, 'International Law and the Nineteenth Century: History of an Illusion' [1996] 17 QLR 99, 100).

99 Among many others, Lauterpacht was one of the spearheads of this reinvention of the periodization of the history of the field with a view to vindicating the uniqueness of his time and his own stature as a figurehead of a new cosmopolitanism and liberalism in international law. See the remarks of Koskenniemi, *Gentle Civilizer of Nations* (Cambridge University Press 2001), 354. On the project of renewal of interwar international lawyers, see D Kennedy, 'International Law and the Nineteenth Century: History of an Illusion' [1996] 17 QLR 99, 110 ("This modern project of renewal through recollection, the ex-post reconstruction of a classical doctrinal system, seemed urgent in the post-war nineteen twenties").

100 See gen Philip Allott, 'Language, Method and the Nature of International Law' [1971] 45 BYBIL 79, 122.

101 This project of reinvention was primarily conducted in academic circles. As Koskenniemi pointed out, most international lawyers of the time continued to participate in practice and international organizations as usual (Martti Koskenniemi, 'History of International Law, World War I to World War II' *Max Planck Encyclopedia of Public International Law* (2011).

and periodization of the early disciplinary histories in order to refute any pedigree with the 19th century international legal thought and practice. These international lawyers, with a view to projecting an image of their time as a rupture, felt that they could not seek the foundations of their century's legal thought in the preceding century but in the 17th century of which the 20th century was to become the heir.[102] In their view, the 20th century shared a pedigree with the 'humanism' of the 17th and 18th century, and not with the 19th century.[103] As a result of this quest for a continuity with a more distance past, the 19th century came to be portrayed as the dark ages of the "political" and of the "sovereign" from which those international lawyers had to heroically emancipate themselves[104] and which had to be quickly forgotten.[105] The role and place of the 19th century were thus completely re-invented to mark the rupture which the 20th century was ought to constitute. This said, subject to this above alteration,[106] late 19th century and 20th century's linear

102 It should be made clear that the exceptionalism vindicated by interwar international lawyers did not entail any satisfaction with the interwar period itself. For instance, Lauterpacht qualified the interwar period as "retrogression". See Lauterpacht, 'International Law after the Convenant' in *International Law Collected Papers 2. The Law of the Peace, Part I International Law in General* (CUP 1975) 145. See the remarks of Koskenniemi, *Gentle Civilizer of Nations* (Cambridge University Press 2001), 356. Compare with the depiction of the loss of rights in the interwar period by Hannah Arendt, *Origins of Totalitarianism* (Schocken Books 1951) ch 9.

103 David Kennedy has spoken about the "forgetfulness" about the 19th century (D Kennedy, 'International Law and the Nineteenth Century: History of an Illusion' [1996] 17 QLR 99, 100, 106–107. Kennedy writes: "For today's international lawyer, the nineteenth century seems long ago and far away, in many ways more distant from current problems and reflections than the great publicists of the seventeenth and eighteenth centuries – Hugo Grotius, Franciscus Suarez, Emmerich de Vattel, and the rest. Moreover, the international lawyer's memory of the nineteenth century, as our nineteenth century disciplinary forebearers, is connected only very loosely to anything that happened or was thought between 1800 and 1900" (ibid., 100).

104 On the portrayal of the 19th century and its positivism as a dark age of state-centrism and sovereignty, see the remarks of Koskenniemi, *Gentle Civilizer of Nations* (Cambridge University Press 2001), 355. Compare with Hannah Arendt's depiction of the 19th century, Hannah Arendt, *Origins of Totalitarianism* (Schocken Books 1951) ch 9, esp 291 and 298–299. See also Thomas Kleinlein (n 65) 813.

105 This is very pregnant in Lauterpacht's *The Function of Law in the International Community* (2nd ed, OUP 2011). See the remarks of M Koskenniemi in *Preface*, xxix and xxxvi (ibid.).

106 Regarding the project of reinvention, Martti Koskenniemi writes "The target is not (European) tradition per se, not even the main current of that tradition, Enlightenment thought. Lauterpacht's critical posture is internal to its cosmopolitan and rationalist mainstream and directed at the margins, against the 'metaphysical' or outright 'mystical' doctrines of nationalism, statehood, and sovereignty. (See M Koskenniemi, *Gentle Civilizer of Nations* (Cambridge University Press 2001, 359).

disciplinary histories of international law thrived unchallenged throughout the 20th century.[107] They did even more so as less energy was devoted to the production of disciplinary histories in the second half of the 20th century.[108] The 'historical turn' is the marker that is commonly used to designate the moment the fortune of such linear disciplinary histories that had emerged with the professionalization of the discipline came to end. It is to the various manifestations of this 'historical turn' and the way in which they sought to displace and disrupt common linear disciplinary histories of international law that the attention now turns.

3 The 'Historical Turn' and the Burgeoning of Critical Histories

Before sketching out some of the manifestations of the so-called 'historical turn' and the rise of international lawyers' interest in historiographical debates, a preliminary remark on the idea of 'turn' must be formulated. There always is some degree of oversimplification in disciplinary accounts built in terms of 'turns'.[109] This is especially so as far as the 'historical turn' in international law is concerned. Indeed, it must be acknowledged that the idea of 'historical turn' as a marker is simplistic given the fact that the Enlightenment – that provided its dualistic patterns of thoughts and progress narratives to international law – itself came with an unprecedented historical self-consciousness,[110] even

107 Such a linear history was comforted by the translation the translation of the work of some of the elected founding fathers of international law in non-Western languages. On the translation of Suarez, Vattel, and Wheaton into Chinese, see Alexander Orakhelashvili, 'The relevance of theory and history – the essence and origins of international law' in A Orakhelashvili (ed), *Research Handbook on the Theory and History of International Law* (Elgar 2011) 21–22.

108 Martti Koskenniemi has argued that there was not much professional international legal historiography in the 1970s and 1980s. See Martti Koskenniemi, 'Histories of International Law: Significance and Problems for a Critical View' [2013] 27 Temple International and Comparative Law Journal 215, 217.

109 For a criticisms of discourses in 'turns', see Gary Wilder, 'From Optic to Topic: The Foreclosure Effect of Historiographic Turns' (2012) 117 (3) American Historical Review 723, 730 (discussing the foreclosure of discourses of turns and their conservatism).

110 Hayden White, *Metahistory. The Historical Imagination in the 19th-Century Europe* (Johns Hopkins University Press, 2014), 51 ("The Enlightenment's own posture vis-à-vis historical writing in general was Ironic" ... (It) "did so in full consciousness of the possibility of a choice between so using it and practicing it for its own sake or, as it is said, for itself alone"). See also Michel Foucault, *L'archéologie du savoir* (Gallimard, 1969), p. 23. See also Peter Sloterdijk, *Après Nous le Déluge*, Editions Payot & Rivages, 2016, at 16; Hans-Georg Gadamer, Truth and Method, Bloomsbury, 2013, at xxiii.

though the historical self-consciousness of the Enlightenment was precisely to discontinue the foundational role of the past and built truth-searching in reason and concreteness.[111] The idea of a 'historical turn' as a marker is not without contradictions either, for, while targeting existing linear and progressive disciplinary histories of the field, it constitutes just another linear and progressive narrative about the discipline.[112]

It is submitted here that, notwithstanding such oversimplification and contradictions, one can hardly deny that the end of the 20th century witnessed a rise of interest in historiographical debates about the history of the discipline as well as enhanced suspicion towards the linear mainstream disciplinary histories that had been perpetuated throughout the 20th century.[113] Such change of attitude can be evidenced somewhat empirically. At least to the extent that the amount of scholarly publications that engage with a critique of disciplinary

111 See Claude Levi Strauss, 'The Structural Study of Myth' (1955) 68 (270) The Journal of American Floklore 428; Levi-Strauss, The Savage Mind (University of Chicago Press 1966) ch 1. See also Hayden White, *Metahistory. The Historical Imagination in the 19th-Century Europe* (Johns Hopkins University Press, 2014), 51–52 ("data from the past – everything contained in legend, myth, fable – were excluded as potential evidence for determining the truth about the past").

112 The 'historical turn' has also been presented as an offspring of the linguistic turn and has elected Michel Foucault, Edward Said, Hayden White, and others as its intellectual forebears. See the remarks of, Janne Nijman, Janne Nijman who has called it a turn to "history as theory". See Janne Nijman, 'Seeking Change by Doing History' (Amsterdam University Press, 2018) 9–10. Accessed 15th June 2018 at <https://ssrn.com/abstract=3167708>, at 6.

113 See Anne Orford, 'International Law and the Limits of History' in W Werner and others (eds), *The Law of International Lawyers: Reading Martti Koskenniemi* (CUP 2015) 297 ("International law has always had a deep engagement with the past. Past text and concepts are constantly retrieved and taken up as a resource in international legal argumentation and scholarship. This the 'turn to history' trop marks a turn to history as a method, rather than a turn to history in terms of engaging with the past rather than the present", ibid., 297, 307). This growing interest for the history of international law is also witnessed in relation to private international law. See e.g. Roxana Banu, *Nineteenth-Century Perspectives on Private International Law* (OUP, 2018). It has been said that a historical turn has similarly been witnessed in international relations. For an illustration about the current engagement with the history of international relations, see Duncan Bell, "International Relations: The Dawn of a Historiographical Turn?" 3 British Journal of Politics and International Relations (2001) 115–126; David Armitage, "The Fifty Years' Rift: Intellectual History and International Relations" 1 Modern Intellectual History (2004), 97–109; Brian Schmidt, The Political Discourse of Anarchy: A Disciplinary History of International Relations (Albany, NY: State University of New York Press, 1998); Tim Dunne, Inventing International Society: A History of the English School (London: Macmillan, 1998); Chris Brown, Terry Nardin, and Nicholas Rengger, eds., International Relations in Political Thought: Texts from the Ancient Greeks to the First World War (Cambridge: Cambridge University Press, 2002).

histories of international law and provide counter-narratives plausibly constitute indicators of the historical self-consciousness of the field.[114] More importantly and more decisively, it seems that very few aspects of the linear disciplinary histories invented in the late 19th century and in the beginning of the 20th century – and which have been recalled in the previous section – have been spared by critical histories. Very compelling challenges have been levelled against dominant disciplinary histories of international law.

Unsurprisingly, the 'historical turn' is a multifaceted phenomenon. Some of the manifestations thereof are mentioned here. The 'historical turn' has, for instance, been epitomized by abounding charges against Enlightenment narratives of progress informing the common disciplinary histories[115] and their obfuscation of the wrong that international law is associated with.[116] The very linear character of the common disciplinary histories similarly came under attack as it was claimed that the history of international law should rather been told as "pockmarked by a series of catastrophes and mutations".[117] Likewise, some of the fundamental markers of the discipline came to be questioned.

114 On the idea that the 'historical turn' has attracted less attention in Germany, see Felix Lange, 'The dream of a völkish colonial empire: international law and colonial law during the National Socialist era' (2017) 4 (3) London Review of International Law 343, 344.

115 Matthew Craven, 'Introduction: International Law and Its Histories' in Matthew Craven, Malgosia Fitzmaurice and Maria Vogiatzi (eds), *Time, History and International Law* (Brill 2007), 9; Lessaffer, this volume; D Z Cass, 'Navigating the Newstream: Recent Critical Scholarship in International Law' (1996) 65 (3) Nordic Journal of International Law 341.

116 Luigi Nuzzo, "The Birth of an Imperial Location: Comparative Perspectives on Western Colonialism in China" 31 Leiden Journal of International Law (2018) 569, at 596.

117 N Berman, 'In the Wake of Empire' [1999] 14 American University International Law Review 1515, 1523: ("The genealogical approach rejects this account of international legal history as an ever-advancing dialectic of restatement and renewal. It views international legal history as pockmarked by a series of catastrophes and mutations, as rocked by the countless forms of colonial conquest and anti-colonial resistance"). At p. 1524 he writes: "International legal genealogy rejects linear accounts of the origins and progress of the international community. It recounts the forging of that community through acts of unholy matrimony, through liaisons mostly asymmetrical, even when consensual, and all-too-often irreversibly coercive and massively violent – and usually constructing the power of some patriarch or other". See also John Haskell, 'The Traditions of Modernity within International Law and Governance: Christianity, Liberalism, and Marxism' [2014] 6 Human Rights & Globalization Law Review 29, 37 (discussing the kinship between modernity and linear history as well as the Christian heritage).

For instance, the fatherhood of Grotius,[118] the canonical status of his work,[119] and the cosmopolitan project associated therewith[120] have been severely questioned. Mention must also be made here of the compelling lessons of

118 For a plea to study the precursors of Grotius as Grotius is the heir of a tradition, see Randall Lesaffer, 'International Law and Its History: The Story of an Unrequited Love' in Matthew Craven, Malgosia Fitzmaurice and Maria Vogiatzi (eds), *Time, History and International Law* (Brill 2007) 40; see also José-Manuel Barreto, 'Cerberus: Rethinking Grotius and the Westphalian System' in Martti Koskenniemi, Walter Rech, and Manuel Jimenez Fonseca (eds), *International Law and Empire* (OUP 2017) 154.

119 As was discussed by Simpson, the earlier work by Grotius, and especially *De Jure Praedae*, seem to point in the exact opposite direction of the 20th century progressive narrative which it is supposed to have engendered. In De Jure Praedae of Grotius distinguishes between dates on the basis of their internal politics and moral characteristics. See G Simpson, *Great Powers and Outlaw States. Unequal Sovereigns in their International Legal Order* (CUP, 2004) 4. See also the idea that the modernity of international law started with the Spanish age defended by Bardo Fassbender, 'Peace of Westphalia (1648)' *Max Planck Encyclopedia of Public International Law* (2011) para 19. See also the remarks of J. Haskell, 'Hugo Grotius in the Contemporary Memory of International Law: Secularism, Liberalism, and the Politics of Restatement and Denial' in J M Beneyto, D Kennedy, J Corti Varela and J Haskell (eds), *New approaches to international law: the European and the American experiences* (Asser Press 2012) 123–150.

120 On the idea of Dutch imperialism in the work of Grotius, see José-Manuel Barreto, 'Cerberus: Rethinking Grotius and the Westphalian System' in Martti Koskenniemi, Walter Rech, and Manuel Jimenez Fonseca (eds), *International Law and Empire* (OUP 2017) 158 ("Grotius has not lost his place between the founding fathers of modern international law. He remains inhabiting such an Olympus, yet in another sense or for different reasons. It has been made clear that Grotius is not the founder of international law defined as a system that regulates the affaires between equal and sovereign states. Together with Vitoria, Grotius remains in the selected group of the 'early parents of modern international law', a legal regime that is understood as emerging out of imperialism's needs for legitimation, and that regulated the relations between its subjects, including early modern companies"). On the idea that the writing of Grotius, like those of Gentili and Vattel are construed as justifying "imperial activities of their clients", see Martti Koskenniemi 'Introduction: International Law and Empire – Aspects and Approaches' in Martti Koskenniemi, Walter Rech, and Manuel Jimenez Fonseca (eds), *International Law and Empire* (OUP 2017) 4 (Citing Jonathan Israel, Dutch Primacy in World Trade 1585–1740 (Clarendon 1989) 16–17 and 69–73). For some critique of Grotius as serving the VOC, see Benjamin Straumann, '"Ancient Caesarean Lawyers" in a State of Nature: Roman Tradition and Natural Rights in Hugo Grotius's "De iure praedae"' [2006] 34 Political Theory 328; Renee Jeffery, *Hugo Grotius in International Thought* (Palgrave Macmillan 2006) 6–7; Tarik Kochi, *The Other's War. Recognition and the Violence of Ethics* (Birkbeck Law Press 2009) 59–60. On Grotius and Mercantile Capitalism, see Martti Koskenniemi, "International Law and the Emergence of Mercantile Capitalism: Grotius To Smith" in P.-M. Dupuy and V. Chetail (eds), *The Roots of International Law. Liber Amicorum Peter Haggenmacher* (Nijhoff, 2014), 3. On the criticisms of Grotius for its neo-liberalism, see Monica Garcia-Salmones Rovira, *The Project of Positivism in International Law* (OUP 2013).

the critique of law and empire[121] and, especially those vindicated by the Third World Approaches to International Law (TWAIL) which seek to repudiate the narrative of universality that has accompanied mainstream linear disciplinary histories.[122] The critique of law and empire has itself been the object of counter-critique.[123]

This new surge of critical histories has not only focused on the main markers of the dominant linear disciplinary histories but has also expressed itself through a questioning of some of the periodization and causal sequencing

---

121 Among others, see Martti Koskenniemi, *Gentle Civilizer of Nations* (Cambridge University Press 2001); Martti Koskenniemi, 'Empire and International Law: The Real Spanish Contribution' (2011) 61 (1) University of Toronto Law Journal 1; China Miéville, *Between Equal Rights: A Marxist Theory of International Law* (Haymarket Books 2006). Sundhya Pahuja, "The Postcoloniality of International Law" 46 Harvard International Law Journal (2005) 459; See also Juan Pablo Scarfi, *The Hidden History of International Law in the Americas. Empire and Legal Networks* (OUP 2017). For an attempt to play down the critique of international law and empire, see Andrew Fitzmaurice, 'Liberalism and Empire in Nineteenth-Century International Law' (2012) 117 (1) American Historical Review 122, 138; Liliana Obregon, "Empire, Racial Capitalism and International Law: The Case of Manumitted Haiti and the Recognition Debt", 31 *Leiden Journal of International Law* (2018), 597–615; Felix Lange, 'The dream of a völkish colonial empire: international law and colonial law during the National Socialist era' (2017) 4 (3) London Review of International Law 343; For a discussion of the tension between the universalist project of international law and its imperialism as well as an attempt to overcome this tension, see E Jouannet, 'Universalism and Imperialism: The True-False Paradox of International Law?' (2007) 18 (3) European Journal of International Law 379; E. Tourme-Jouannet, "Des Origines Coloniales du Droit International : A Propos du Droit des Gens Moderne au 18ème Siècle", in P.-M. Dupuy and V. Chetail (eds), *The Roots of International Law. Liber Amicorum Peter Haggenmacher* (Nijhoff, 2014), 648. Compare with the German jurists' Interwar critique of League of Nations as empire (see Martti Koskenniemi 'Introduction: International Law and Empire – Aspects and Approaches' in Martti Koskenniemi, Walter Rech, and Manuel Jimenez Fonseca (eds), *International Law and Empire* (OUP 2017) 3. See Felix Lange, 'The dream of a völkish colonial empire: international law and colonial law during the National Socialist era' (2017) 4 (3) London Review of International Law 343.

122 See eg Antony Anghie, *Imperialism, Sovereignty, and the Making of International Law* (Cambridge University Press 2005); Makau Mutua, 'What is TWAIL?' 94 American Society of International Law Proceedings 31; Antony Anghie, 'The Evolution of International Law: colonial and postcolonial realities' (2006) 27 (5) Third World Quarterly 740; B S Chimni, 'Third World Approaches to International Law: A Manifesto' (2006) 8 International Community Law Review 18; Makau Mutua, 'Savages, Victims and Saviors: The Metaphor of Human Rights' (2001) 42 (1) Harvard International Law Journal 201. For one of the foundational work of TWAIL, see E Said, *Orientalism* (Routledge 1978).

123 See e.g. Shotaro Hamamoto, 'A propose de deux clichés sur l'histoire du droit international en Asie de l'Est : une reconsidération de l'ordre mondial chinois et du discours de traités inégaux' in in P.-M. Dupuy and V. Chetail (eds), *The Roots of International Law. Liber Amicorum Peter Haggenmacher* (Nijhoff, 2014), 743–756.

around which dominant linear disciplinary histories were articulated.[124] Among others, it is worth mentioning the severe contestation of the above-mentioned historical narrative whereby the 20th century's international law is meant to constitute a rupture from the 19th century but to continue 17th century's humanism.[125] This is for instance the challenge vindicated by David Kennedy who has argued that the modernity of the 20th century and its main paradigmatic foundations are all inherited from the 19th century which 20th century's international law perpetuates.[126] Although he argues that part of the continuity between the 19th century and 20th century has been discontinued somewhere in the second half of the 20th century, Martti Koskenniemi has similarly put forward a nuanced periodization[127] and claimed that some of the main international law's figures of the 20th century espoused "nineteenth-century liberal sentiments"[128] and that the 19th century and 20th century ought to be read together as one epoch in terms of international legal thought.[129]

---

124 See generally Alexandra Kemmerer 'We do not need to always look to Westphalia ... A Conversation with Martti Koskenniemi and Anne Orford' [2015] 17 Journal of the History of International Law 1. On the idea that innovative narrativization lies in the forming and imposing of new periods, see Oliver Diggelman, 'The Periodization of the History of International Law' in Bardo Fassbender and Anne Peters (eds), *The Oxford Handbook of the History of International Law* (OUP, 2012) 996, 998

125 See section 2.

126 D Kennedy 'International Law and the Nineteenth Century: History of an Illusion' [1996] 17 QLR 99, 102–103. David Kennedy has challenged the very idea of the nineteen century as "the break which opened the modern period at the beginning of (the last) century (ibid., 99).

127 On the idea that Koskenniemi's Gentle Civilizer of Nations comes with a new periodization, see Diggelman, 'The Periodization of the History of International Law' in Bardo Fassbender and Anne Peters (eds), *The Oxford Handbook of the History of International Law* (OUP, 2012) 996, 998. For some criticisms of periodization of Koskenniemi and the claim that Koskenniemi's demarcation is "rhetorical ploy", see Amnon Lev, 'The transformation of international law in the 19th century' in A Orakhelashvili (ed), *Research Handbook on the Theory and History of International Law* (Elgar 2011) 112.

128 Koskenniemi, *Gentle Civilizer of Nations* (Cambridge University Press 2001), 358.

129 Part of Kennedy's and Koskenniemi's claim of a continuity between the 19th and 20th centuries lies in the fact that the attacks against the alleged positivism and state-centricism of the former were launched in the name of science and empirics. See eg Lauterpacht, 'The Function of Law in the International Community' (2nd edition, OUP 2011) 95. See M. Koskenniemi, *Gentle Civilizer of Nations* (Cambridge University Press 2001), 365: "Lauterpacht's attack was conducted in the name of the universal principles of science: logical consistency and correspondence with facts". "Lauterpacht is able to attack voluntarist positivism on its own terrain of scientific factuality without having to resort to the moralizing rhetoric of naturalism or the formalism of the pure theory of law" (ibid.).

Steiger has proposed a similar challenge.[130] All these authors have traced the pedigree of contemporary international legal thought to a more immediate past instead of the remote humanist past in which interwar international lawyers in particular had found their own roots.[131]

The foregoing are just a few of the ways in which the so-called 'historical turn' has materialized over the last two decades. A final remark is warranted about the moment of this 'historical turn'. It can be argued that the multiplication of critical histories in international legal scholarship initiated two decades ago was not fully fortuitous. In fact, once international lawyers accept that international law is itself literary composition – which is one of the main lessons of critical thought – it does not take much to realize the limits of the linear disciplinary histories with which the international legal literature had always been awash till then. In fact, giving a meaning to past texts, doctrines, concepts, and practices and organizing them to support a legal claim in the present is not different from the narrativization of a formless past and the systematization of past events according to one's agenda, ideology and perceptions of what one's audience is amenable to. In that sense, the so-called 'historical turn' in international legal literature can be seen as a very natural corollary of the anti-liberal and anti-modern attitude that made a tangible appearance in international legal thought a decade earlier.[132] And yet, as is argued in the next section, the kinship between the 'historical turn' and critical legal theory has not sufficed to make such new critical histories radically critical.

---

130 Steiger, 'From the International Law of Christianity to the International Law of the World Citizens' [2001] 3 Journal of the History of International Law 180.

131 For his part, and in a different vein, Lesaffer also seeks to play down the rupturing character of the 20th century and yet vindicate a much older pedigree than Grotius by finding a genealogy with Francisco Vitoria (Randall Lesaffer, 'The Grotian Tradition Revisited: Change and Continuity in the History of International Law' (2003) 73 (1) British Yearbook of International Law (2002) 103, 137). For yet another attempt to make the 19th century pivotal but short of domination and because of a transformation that happened in the wake of the French Revolution, see Amnon Lev, 'The transformation of international law in the 19th century' in A Orakhelashvili (ed), *Research Handbook on the Theory and History of International Law* (Elgar 2011) 121.

132 See however B S Chimni's contestation of the idea that Koskenniemi's historiographical work leaves his earlier work on the structure of international legal argumentation intact. Chimni argues that one cannot add post facto history to structure. See B S Chimni, *International Law and World Order. A Critique of Contemporary Approaches* (2nd ed, CUP 2017) 322.

4 The Continuous Complacency of Contemporary Critical Histories

This section seeks to shed light on the complacency of the critical histories that have been flourishing since the 'historical turn' in international law. In particular, it is argued here that the disruption and displacement envisaged by contemporary critical histories remains hindered by their articulation around the very same markers, periodization and causal sequencing of those narratives they seek to disrupt. By confining themselves to the very markers, periodization and causal sequencing of the linear disciplinary histories with which they take aim, these new critical histories uphold more than they disrupt or displace.

It must be acknowledged that claims about the complacency of contemporary critical histories are not unheard of. Those earlier charges mostly pertained to the contextualism that has informed many such critical histories[133] or their attachment to juridical thinking.[134] Such strictures have also drawn on the extent to which these critical histories have reinforced the modern

133 See the remarks of Anne Orford about the loss in critical attitude that may be brought about by the turn to history and its embrace of contextualism. See Anne Orford, 'International Law and the Limits of History' in W Werner and others (eds), *The Law of International Lawyers: Reading Martti Koskenniemi* (CUP 2015) esp 301–306. (Anne Orford sees pleas in favour of a more rigourous contextualism as well as the necessity to use historical protocols as being conducive to conservatism. See also Anne Orford, 'On international legal method' [2013] 1 London Review of International Law 166, 170–177. See also the remarks of Matthew Craven, 'Introduction: International Law and Its Histories' in Matthew Craven, Malgosia Fitzmaurice and Maria Vogiatzi (eds), *Time, History and International Law* (Brill 2007) 12–13; Martti Koskenniemi came to nuance his earlier allegedly contextualist approach, see Martti Koskenniemi, 'Histories of International Law: Significance and Problems for a Critical View' [2013] 27 Temple International and Comparative Law Journal 215, 229–232. For some remarks seeking to salvage the merits of Skinner's contextualist school, see Janne Nijman who has called it a turn to "history as theory". See Janne Nijman, 'Seeking Change by Doing History' (Amsterdam University Press, 2018) 9–10. Accessed 15th June 2018 at <https://ssrn.com/abstract=3167708>, at 10–13. For some resilient plea for contextualism despite the critique see Wolfgang Preiser, 'History of International Law, Basic Questions and Principles' *Max Planck Encyclopedia of Public International Law* (2007) para 8. For general observations on this debate see Thomas Kleinlein (n 65) 811, or more recently, see Christopher N Warren, 'History, Literature, and Authority in International Law' in Maksymilian Del Mar, Bernadette Meyler, and Simon Stern (eds), *Oxford Handbook of Law and Humanities* (OUP, forthcoming). See also Kate Purcell, 'Faltering at the Critical Turn to History: 'Juridical Thinking' in International Law and Genealogy as History, Critique, and Therapy' (2016) Jean Monnet Working Paper Series, JMWP 02/15, 17–27.

134 For a discussion of this point, see Kate Purcell, 'Faltering at the Critical Turn to History: 'Juridical Thinking' in International Law and Genealogy as History, Critique, and Therapy' (2016) Jean Monnet Working Paper Series, JMWP 02/15.

"status of history as a master discipline dedicated to producing the objective truth about the past".[135] The claim of complacency that is developed in this article is distinct from these previous objections as it builds on the finding of a confinement of critical histories to the very same markers, periodization and causal sequencing as the linear disciplinary histories they take aim at, which has arguably been the object of little attention.

The specific charge that critical histories found in the international legal literature are complacent goes as follows. As was discussed in section 1 above, historical narratives are constructions providing meaning to past events, texts, figures, and practices by virtue of markers, causal sequencing and periodization. This means that debunking a historical narrative accordingly entails a repudiation of the markers, periodization, and causal sequencing on which it is built. And yet, in historiographical works that have been produced since the 'historical turn', the disruption and displacement of dominant historical disciplinary narratives about international law have, in practice, entailed the application of the very same past events, texts, figures and practices around which the historical narratives under attack were molded. Although attempting some significant nuances, the critical histories that have been flourishing after the 'historical turn' in international legal scholarship have fallen short of renewing the markers, periodization and causal sequencing which they have been built around. Historical critique has just been a matter of 'applying" differently the very categories around which mainstream historical narratives are articulated, critical histories often being reduced to a variant of the linear disciplinary histories that they are engaging with. Although they seek to disrupt accepted causal sequencing and expose contingency, it seems that counterfactual histories have similarly remained confined to the very categories of linear histories of international law.[136]

A few illustrations of the complacency – as it is understood here – of the critical histories produced in international legal scholarship over the last two decades can be provided here. Such complacency expresses itself, for instance, in the fact that the historiographical imagination of international lawyers continues to revolve around the same genealogical inquiries, namely whether Gentili, Vitoria, Grotius, Vattel, Lauterpacht, etc. are the spearheads, the heroes, the founding fathers, the (re-)inventers, or the heirs of the Western

---

135 Anne Orford, 'International Law and the Limits of History' in W Werner and others (eds), *The Law of International Lawyers: Reading Martti Koskenniemi* (CUP 2015) 308. On this question, see section 6 below.

136 See Ingo Venzke, 'What If? Counterfactual (Hi)Stories of International Law' (2016) Amsterdam Center for International Law No 2016–21; Amsterdam Law School Research Paper No 2016–66. Accessed 16th June 2018 at SSRN: https://ssrn.com/abstract=2881226.

Enlightenment and (pre- or post-) modern international law. Said differently, and although international lawyers today are prone to recognize that Gentili, Grotius or Vattel may not have been the cosmopolitan humanitarians with which their status of fathers of international law endowed them,[137] such critical histories remain historical narratives about Gentili, Vitoria, Grotius, Vattel, Lauterpacht, etc.[138] It could even be argued that the critical discussions of some of the heroes may well have contributed to their further canonization, for critically engaging with those considered the "fathers" only reinforces their fatherly place in disciplinary histories. A good example thereof is provided by the numerous and well-known critical engagements with the legacy of Lauterpacht that have been witnessed in the literature. Indeed, while showing the limits and contradictions of Lauterpacht's scientific cosmopolitanism,[139] such studies have inevitably led to a further consolidation of Lauterpacht stature in the linear disciplinary histories of the field.[140] It could even be ventured that Lauterpacht was maybe not perceived as much a pivotal figure as he is today until the 'historical turn' and the critical engagement therewith.[141]

In the same vein, it is conspicuous that historiographical debates in international legal scholarship are restricted to the same periodical controversies articulated around the scholastic, the pre-modern, Westphalia, the Enlightenment, the modern, colonization, the 19th, the interwar period, the post-League of Nations, the post-second-world war, decolonization, the cold war, the post-cold war, etc.[142] It could be contended that even the agendas debated in such historiographical literature are identical: humanism,

137 See n 112.

138 See eg Onuma Yasuaki, *International Law in a Transcivilizational World* (CUP 2017) 11.

139 On Lauterpacht's liberalism and modernism, see the remarks of M Koskenniemi, *Gentle Civilizer of Nations* (Cambridge University Press 2001), 357.

140 For an example, see eg the introduction of M Koskenniemi in Hirsch Lauterpacht, *The Function of Law in the International Community* (2nd edition, 2011). Koskenniemi writes: "The Function of Law is the most important English-language book on international law in the 20th century" (ibid., xlvii). See also M Koskenniemi, *Gentle Civilizer of Nations* (Cambridge University Press 2001), 355–364.

141 Compare with the extent to which the discourse over the Orient is constitutive of the Occident; see E Said, *Orientalism* (Routledge 1978) 13.

142 For an illustration of the use of 1648 in historical critique, see D Kennedy 'Primitive Legal Scholarship' [1986] 27 Harvard International Law Journal 1, 1–2. See the remarks of Randall Lesaffer, 'International Law and Its History: The Story of an Unrequited Love' in Matthew Craven, Malgosia Fitzmaurice and Maria Vogiatzi (eds), *Time, History and International Law* (Brill 2007) 40 (He writes that even if myth of Westphalia has been debunked, it continues to be restated again and again). See also the remarks of Martti Koskenniemi, 'Histories of International Law: Dealing with Eurocentrism', lecture on 16 November 2011, 5.

cosmopolitanism, modernism, state-centricism, voluntarism, colonialism, hegemony, capitalism, etc.

Another significant manifestation of the complacency of these critical histories is their continuous rehabilitation of the distinction between the past and the present.[143] In fact, despite widely recognizing that histories are political interventions whereby the past is reshaped and mobilized to support action in the present,[144] many of such critical histories and their counter-narrative continue to presuppose a stable and formed past, albeit one that is different from those promoted in linear historical narratives. Whilst recognizing that the past that is projected by such studies is simply not the one international lawyers learnt through linear disciplinary histories but one that is dirty, gloomy, violent, and unjust,[145] these critical histories still presuppose a past that is out there and that international lawyers are bound to receive. In that sense, critical histories witnessed after the 'historical turn' are as modern as the linear disciplinary histories they seek to disrupt or displace.[146]

A similar observation must be formulated in relation to the many recent critical histories that have very appropriately moved the attention away from the writings of Western jurists and the practice of international law in Western locations, opened new horizons, and provided a wealth of new materials and insights.[147] Despite their merits, many of them have confirmed the complacency of critical histories as they have continued to resort to markers,

---

143 In the same sense, see Rose Parfitt, The Spectre of Sources, 25 European Journal of International Law (2014)297–306, at 304. A somewhat similar claim has already been made by Anne Orford who contends that such critical histories reinforces the power of discplinary history-writing dedicated to the creation of an 'effet du réél'. See Anne Orford, 'International Law and the Limits of History' in W Werner and others (eds), *The Law of International Lawyers: Reading Martti Koskenniemi* (CUP 2015) 308: "In performing these 'more or less confident acts of historicization', these 'critical' histories ironically shored up the status of history as a master discipline dedicated to producing the objective truth about the past. Even as these histories reveal the constructed nature of the disciplines they were critiquing, they reaffirmed 'the power of history as a disciplinary practice".

144 Rose Parfitt, The Spectre of Sources, 25 European Journal of International Law (2014) 297–306, at 305. Anne Orford, 'International Law and the Limits of History' in W Werner and others (eds), *The Law of International Lawyers: Reading Martti Koskenniemi* (CUP 2015).

145 See N Berman, In the Wake of Empire 14 American University International Law Review (1999) 1521, at 1524.

146 See gen. Hayden White, Hayden White, *Metahistory. The Historical Imagination in the 19th-Century Europe* (Johns Hopkins University Press, 2014), 51.

147 See the remarks of Lauren Benton, "Made in Empire: Finding the History of International Law in Imperial Locations", 31 *Leiden Journal of International Law* (2018), 473–478.

periodization and causal sequencing all located in the West.[148] This charge is not unheard of. It had already been raised against the first post-colonial histories of international law[149] which, despite their attempt to provincialize Europe, have been criticized for reclaiming non-Western contributions within mainstream histories of international law.[150] It is also a charge leveled against those works that seek to emphasize non-European perspectives,[151] for they re-center non-Western locations and perspectives within a very Eurocentric history and through European markers, periodization, and causal sequencing.[152]

It is argued here that the same holds with respect to recent critical histories that, notwithstanding their very valuable disruptive insights, continue to rely on markers, periodization and causal sequencing of histories of international law built around roman law, the scholastic, the *droit public de l'Europe*,

148 This has been a criticism levelled by B.S. Chimni against the work of Koskenniemi (BS Chimni, International Law and World Order. A Critique of Contemporary Approaches (2nd ed., CUP, 2017), 322 and 327–339. See also Matthew Craven, Introduction: International Law and Its Histories in Matthew Craven, Malgosia Fitzmaurice and Maria Vogiatzi (eds), Time, History and International Law, Brill 2007 1, at 12–13.

149 See e.g. C. H. Alexandrowicz, An Introduction to the History of the Law of Nations in the East Indies (Clarendon, 1967); C. H. Alexandrowicz, *The Law of Nations in Global History* (OUP, 2017); Taslim Olawale Elías, Africa and the Development of International Law (Sijthoff, 1972) R. P. Anand, Origin and Development of the Law of the Sea: History of International Law Revisited (Martinus Nijhoff, 1983); For an overview of these works by the first generation of TWAIL scholars, see Arnulf Becker Lorca, Eurocentricism in the History of International Law, in Bardo Fassbender and Anne Peters (eds), The Oxford Handbook of the History of International Law (OUP, 2012) 1034; Liliana Obregon, 'Marti Koskenniemi's Critique of Eurocentricism in International Law', in A. Galan, M. de Hoon, and W. Werner (eds), *The Law of International Lawyers: Reading Martti Koskenniemi* (CUP, 2017) 360.

150 This is a charge made by Yasuaki Onuma, International Law in a Transcivilizational World (CUP, 2017) at 13; Onuma Yasuaki, 'When Was the Law of International Society Born – An Inquiry of the History of International Law from an Intercivilizational Perspective', 2 Journal of History of International Law (2000) 1, at 61. See the remarks of, at 1047–1048. A similar charge has been made against.

151 On this type of charge, see Liliana Obregon's comments on the occasion of her interview of Martti Koskenniemi reproduced in Liliana Obregon, 'Martti Koskenniemi's Critique of Eurocentricism in International Law', in A. Galan, M. de Hoon, and W. Werner (eds), *The Law of International Lawyers: Reading Martti Koskenniemi* (CUP, 2017) 360, 374–384 and esp. 378.

152 A good example thereof is provided by C. H. Alexandrowicz who sought to redeem non-Western practice by showing that Grotius had been influenced by Indian Ocean maritime traditions. See C.H. Alexandrowicz, 'Grotius and India' reproduced in C. H. Alexandrowicz, *The Law of Nations in Global History* (OUP, 2017), pp. 113–120. For a criticism of that claim, see D. Armitage and J. Pitts, " 'This Modern Grotius': An Introduction to the Life and Thought of C.H. Alexandrowicz", in C. H. Alexandrowicz, *The Law of Nations in Global History* (OUP, 2017), pp. 28–29.

the reformation, the Peace of Westphalia, the Enlightenment, the 19th and 20th century, the encounter with European imperialism, etc.[153] In such works, non-Western contexts and practices remain treated as "peripheral"[154] and accounted for as a response to (or an encounter with) European or Western international law.[155] What is more, some of these critical histories, whilst lamenting the resilience of the colonial project and the mirage of universality, still pursue the project of a universal international law according to a very European idea of universality.[156]

The same conservatism can be witnessed in the – now very common – critique of law and empire.[157] As far as law and empire is concerned, it must be acknowledged that approaching non-Western practices and contexts as peripheral and resorting to Western markers and periodization[158] is inevitable

---

153 See e.g. A. B. Lorca, *Mestizo International Law: A Global Intellectual History 1841–1933* (Cambridge University Press, 2014) or Onuma Yasuaki, *International Law in a Transcivilizational World* (CUP, 2017), 11. On this point, see the remarks of Martti Koskenniemi, The Case for Comparative International Law, 20 Finnish Yearbook of International Law (2009) 1, at 4.

154 In the same vein, see Arnulf Becker Lorca, Eurocentricism in the History of International Law, in Bardo Fassbender and Anne Peters (eds), *The Oxford Handbook of the History of International Law* (OUP, 2012) 1034, at 1054. It is interesting to note that Koskenniemi has tried to tone this down in M. Koskenniemi, The Case for Comparative International Law 20 Finnish Yearbook of International Law (2009), 1–8.

155 This is also a criticism made by Mohammad Shahabuddin, "The 'standard of civilization' in international law: Intellectual perspectives from pre-war Japan" 32 *Leiden Journal of International Law* (2019) 13–32. See also See also Maiko Meguro, "Backlash against international law by the East? How the concept of 'transplantation' helps us to better understand reception processes of international law", Völkerrechtsblog, 11 January 2019, available at https://voelkerrechtsblog.org/backlash-against-international-law-by-the-east/.

156 Speaking of the work of Bedjaoui, Anand, and Elias, Liliana Obregon argues that this first general of TWAIL scholars viewed the solution to international law's Eurocentricism as the need to make it 'truly universal'. See Liliana Obregon, 'Marti Koskenniemi's Critique of Eurocentricism in International Law', in A. Galan, M. de Hoon, and W. Werner (eds), *The Law of International Lawyers: Reading Martti Koskenniemi* (CUP, 2017) 360, at 373. See also the remarks of Sundhya Pahuja, "The Postcoloniality of International Law" 46 *Harvard International Law Journal* (2005) 459, at 464 (who argues that decolonisation can be construed as the granting of a formal legal status to entities to render them commensurable with the current forms of international law). See also the remarks of Martti Koskenniemi, The Case for Comparative International Law, 20 Finnish Yearbook of International Law (2009) 1, at 4.

157 For an overview of the recent trends in the literature on international law and empire, see Lauren Benton, "Made in Empire: Finding the History of International Law in Imperial Locations", 31 *Leiden Journal of International Law* (2018), 473–478.

158 See however the (neo-Marxist) periodization of international law proposed by Chimni who distinguishes between Old Colonialism (1500–1760, New Colonialism (1760–1875),

as long as the critique of law and empire targets Western imperialism, the reassertions of the West and the exclusion of the non-West through legal categories and practices. And yet, it is argued here that such critical studies, just like all recent critical histories, ought not to remain confined to European or Western imperialism.

Critical histories that actually do away with Eurocentric markers, periodization and causal sequencing are scarce.[159] Among the few actual departures from Eurocentric markers, periodization and causal sequencing,[160] mention can be made of the more recent Luis Eslava, Michael Fakhri, and Vasuki Nesiah's *Bandung, Global History and International Law. Critical Pasts and Pending Futures*,[161] Mohammad Shahabuddin's *The 'standard of civilization' in international law: Intellectual perspectives from pre-war Japan*,[162] and, possibly, Robert Kolb's *Esquisse d'un droit international public des anciennes cultures extra européennes*.[163] For the rest, most critical histories at work in the

---

Imperialism (1875–1945), Neocolonialism (1945–1985), Global Imperialism (1985) see Chimni, pp. 479–524.

159 See e.g. Shotaro Hamamoto, "A Propos de Deux Clichés sur l'Histoire du Droit International en Asie de l'Est : Une Reconsidération de l'Ordre Mondial Chinois et du Discours de Traités Inégaux" in P.-M. Dupuy and V. Chetail (eds), *The Roots of International Law. Liber Amicorum Peter Haggenmacher* (Nijhoff, 2014), 743. See the few other examples mentioned by Arnulf Becker Lorca, Eurocentricism in the History of International Law, in Bardo Fassbender and Anne Peters (eds), *The Oxford Handbook of the History of International Law* (OUP, 2012) 1034, 1044–1048.

160 Although still trying to redeem non-Western practice through Western heroes and concepts, C.H. Alexandrowicz has tried to propose a new periodization in the history of international law that does away with the Peace of Westphalia and is centered on 1815, that is the time, not only of the Congress of Vienna but also the monet when the Kingdom of Poland was created. According to Alexandrowicz, this milestone is what allows the distinction between pre-nineteenth century law of nations based on natural law and universality and the positivist and European conception of international law. On this aspect of Alexandrowicz' work, see D. Armitage and J. Pitts, " 'This Modern Grotius': An Introduction to the Life and Thought of C.H. Alexandrowicz", in C. H. Alexandrowicz, *The Law of Nations in Global History* (OUP, 2017), p. 19.

161 Cambridge University Press, 2017.

162 32 *Leiden Journal of International Law* (2019) 13–32 (focusing on the pre-existing hierarchical order in the Far East and highlighting the relevance of non-European regional order in the discourse on international legal history). For a criticism of the use of sources by Shahabuddin, see Maiko Meguro, "Backlash against international law by the East? How the concept of 'transplantation' helps us to better understand reception processes of international law", Völkerrechtsblog, 11 January 2019, available at https://voelkerrechtsblog.org/backlash-against-international-law-by-the-east/.

163 *Esquisse d'un droit international public des anciennes cultures extra européennes. Amérique précolombienne, Iles polynésiennes, Afrique noire, sous-continent indien, Chine et régions limitrophes* (Pedone, 2010). The work of Kolb is meant to continue the work on

literature since the 'historical turn', notwithstanding their irrefutable insightfulness and sophistication, boil down to variants of the very same markers, periodization and causal sequencing as the ones on which dominant linear disciplinary narratives are built.

5 The Impossibility of Critical Historiography and the Idea of Radical Historical Critique

The claim that many of the critical histories that have been flourishing since the 'historical turn' in international law find themselves confined to the very markers, periodization and causal sequencing of those narratives they are trying to question refers to a theoretical phenomenon that is not unheard of, especially in relation to a critique meant to be primarily internal. For instance, such confinement is what Barthes famously identified as the "tragedy" of writing[164] which permeates any revolutionary move.[165] Theodor Adorno made a similar claim about the voracity of any concept that he sees as creating a totality which draws everything into it, tolerates nothing outside its domain, and translates everything in its own terms, even contradictions to it.[166] In the same vein, Hanna Arendt showed how revolutionaries are bound to recuperate and draw on a faraway past with a view to justifying the uniqueness of

non-Western international law initiated by Wolfgang Preiser. On the ambition of such approach to history, see the remarks of R. Kolb, "Considérations sur le droit international public des anciennes cultures extra-européennes", in in P.-M. Dupuy and V. Chetail (eds), *The Roots of International Law. Liber Amicorum Peter Haggenmacher* (Nijhoff, 2014), 673–709. It must however be stressed that the tone and presentation of this work remains very Eurocentric as those other experiences of international law are situated by reference to modern European international law.

164 « l'écrivain reconnaît la vaste fraicheur du monde présent mais pour en rendre compte, il ne dispose que d'une langue splendide et more, devant sa page blanche, au moment de choisir les mots qui doivent franchement signaler sa place dans l'Histoire et témoigner qu'il en assume les données, il observe une disparité tragique entre ce qu'il fait et ce qu'il voit » (R. Barthes, Le degré zéro de l'écriture, Editions du Seuil, 1972, p. 66).

165 ".... tout situation révolutionaire, dont l'ambiguité fondamentale est qu'il faut bien que la Révolution puise dans ce qu'elle veut détruire l'image même de ce qu'elle veut posséder ». « Comme l'art moderne dans son entier, l'écriture litéraire porte à la fois l'aliénation de l'Histoire et le rêve de l'Histoire » (R. Barthes, Le degré zéro de l'écriture, Editions du Seuil, 1972, p. 67).

166 See gen. Theodor W. Adorno, *Negative Dialectics* (Translated by E.B. Ashton) (Routledge, 1973). On this aspect of Adorno's work, see also the remarks of Frederic Jameson, Late Marxism. Adorno or the Persistence of the Dialectic (Verso, 2007), 20–21 and 25–34

their revolutionary moment and their rupture with a more immediate past.[167] In the context of critical historiography, this is a contention that has famously been articulated by Alasdair McIntyre as well.[168] Judith Butler has similarly argued that the performativity of any critical performance in the present is always dependent on the mobilization of a certain past and of a normative heritage.[169] Hayden White more specifically demonstrated how every discipline is made up of (and organized around) a set of restrictions on thoughts and imagination.[170] The finding of a confinement of critique to the categories and vocabularies of its object has been heard in critical legal literature too.[171] It is thus common to recognize some inevitable degree of conservatism in critique that is primarily internal, including in historical critique. This article is not the place to revisit the question of the limits of internal critique in general. It thus limits itself to a few observations on the possibility and impossibility of critical histories about international law.

Before further shedding light on the complacency of critical histories in international law, it must preliminary be acknowledged that international lawyers interested in critical historical inquiries have shown awareness for critical histories' complacency and their rehabilitation of the markers, periodization and causal sequencing of linear disciplinary histories as well as the Eurocentric character of their inquiries.[172] Yet, it is noteworthy that some of

---

167 This is a way in which one could construe the French and American Revolutions in the 18th century as they sought to draw on Antiquity and earlier ideas of the Republic. See the critical remarks of Hannah Arendt, *On Violence* (Houghton Mifflin Harcourt 1970) 237–238. In the same vein, see the remarks of Harold J. Berman, *Law and Revolution. The Formation of the Western Legal Tradition* (Harvard University Press, 1983), 29.

168 Alasdair MacIntyre, *After Virtue: A Study in Moral Theory* (3rd ed, Duckworth 2007).

169 Judith Butler, 'Critically Queer' (1993) 1 (1) GLQ 17, 24 (she argues that performativity "consists in a reiteration of norms which precede, constraint, and exceed the performer and in that sense, cannot be taken as the fabrication of the performer's 'will' or 'choice'; further, what is 'performed' works to conceal, if not disavow, what remains opaque, unconscious, un-performable. The reduction of performativity to performance would be a mistake".

170 Hayden White, *Tropics of Discourse: Essays in Cultural Criticism* (John Hopkins University Press, 1978) 126–127.

171 Pierre Schlag, '"Le Hors de Texte, C'est Moi" The Politics of Form and the Domestication of Deconstruction' [1990] 11 Cardozo Law Review 1631, at 1631.

172 Martti Koskenniemi, 'Histories of International Law: Significance and Problems for a Critical View' [2013] 27 Temple International and Comparative Law Journal 215, 223. See also Martti Koskenniemi, 'The Case for Comparative International Law' [2009] 20 Finnish Yearbook of International Law 1, 4; B S Chimni, *International Law and World Order. A Critique of Contemporary Approaches* (2nd ed, CUP 2017) 322, 327–339; Arnulf Becker Lorca, 'Eurocentricism in the History of International Law' in Bardo Fassbender and Anne Peters (eds), *The Oxford Handbook of the History of International Law* (OUP 2012) 1034, 1044–1048.

those international lawyers having recognized the complacency of their historiographical inquiries have simultaneously been prompt to concede the ineluctability thereof.[173] This is the case of Martti Koskenniemi.[174] For him, international lawyers cannot deny their debt to their predecessors in terms of histories.[175] He has also pointed out that a total rejection of the categories and vocabularies of preceding histories would be as reductive[176] and that, as a result of such a rejection, international lawyers would deprive themselves of shared historical associates" and "shared imagination".[177] According to him, the European pedigree of the vocabularies targeted by critical histories as well as the terms, vocabularies, and categories of such critical histories cannot be unmade.[178] This is why he came to expressed some resignation as to the impossibility to avoid some degree of Eurocentricism in critical histories,[179] even acknowledging that a critique of Eurocentricism appears to arise from European preoccupations and political beliefs.[180]

In the light of the preceding remarks on the limits of internal critique, Martti Koskenniemi's resignation to some degree of conservatism of historical critique is not unwarranted. As was mentioned above, there are compelling reasons why critique confines itself to the very terms, categories, and vocabularies of the narratives it seeks to disrupt or displace. In particular, one must

173 See e.g. Emmanuelle Tourme-Jouannet, "Des Origines Coloniales du Droit International: A Propos du Droit des Gens Moderne au 18ème Siècle", in P.-M. Dupuy and V. Chetail (eds), *The Roots of International Law. Liber Amicorum Peter Haggenmacher* (Nijhoff, 2014), 648, at 670 ("Comme dans n'importe quel domaine, le contre-récit sur le droit international se condamne en effet à reproduire ce qu'il dénonce").

174 For a thorough discussion of Martti Koskenniemi's take on Eurocentricism, see Liliana Obregon, 'Martti Koskenniemi's Critique of Eurocentricism in International Law', in A. Galan, M. de Hoon, and W. Werner (eds), *The Law of International Lawyers: Reading Martti Koskenniemi* (CUP, 2017) 360, esp. 374–384.

175 Martti Koskenniemi, 'Histories of International Law: Significance and Problems for a Critical View' [2013] 27 Temple International and Comparative Law Journal 215, 216.

176 Koskenniemi (ibid., 224).

177 Martti Koskenniemi, 'A History of International Law Histories' in Bardo Fassbender and Anne Peters, *The Oxford Handbook of International Law* (OUP 2012) 945.

178 Martti Koskenniemi, The Case for Comparative International Law, 20 Finnish Yearbook of International Law (2009) 1, at 4. See also Martti Koskenniemi's remarks on the occasion of the interview conducted by Liliana Obregon and reproduced in Liliana Obregon, 'Martti Koskenniemi's Critique of Eurocentricism in International Law', in A. Galan, M. de Hoon, and W. Werner (eds), *The Law of International Lawyers: Reading Martti Koskenniemi* (CUP, 2017) 360, esp. 377–384.

179 Martti Koskenniemi, 'The Case for Comparative International Law' [2009] 20 Finnish Yearbook of International Law (2009) 1, 5.

180 Martti Koskenniemi, 'Histories of International Law: Significance and Problems for a Critical View' [2013] 27 Temple International and Comparative Law Journal 215, 222.

acknowledge that the very concept of international law creates, as Adorno would put it, a historical totality that draws everything into itself, even counter-narratives and contestation.[181] And yet, it is submitted here that the possible ineluctability of the totality of the concept of international law and the corresponding limits of historical critique does not necessarily need to end with imprisonment and a confinement to the same markers, periodization and causal sequencing.[182] The unavoidability of the confinement of critical histories to the markers, periodization and causal sequencing of linear disciplinary histories still raises a number of questions, especially when it comes to the very breadth of the 'historical turn' discussed here and of the critical histories so commonly celebrated these days.

It is argued here that the abovementioned resignation to complacency is not the only fate of international lawyers interested in critical histories. Three observations are now formulated on the consequences of a confinement of international lawyers' critical histories to the markers, periodization and causal sequencing of dominant linear disciplinary histories and on the incapacity of historiography to host radical historical critique. Building on these three observations, the very idea of a radical historical critique is then substantiated.

The first observation pertains to the repression which the abovementioned complacency of critical histories brings about. In fact, one should be aware that upholding the disciplinary histories' markers, periodization, and causal sequencing not only comes with very strong limitations as to how international lawyers can experience historical self-consciousness but also entails repression. In particular, the constant and uninterrupted reproduction of variants of the common markers, periodization, causal sequencing of linear histories of the discipline bars the possibility of developing alternative histories as well as creating new form-giving and meaning-giving narratives about the past.[183] It is argued here that the impossibility of reinventing another past amounts to a form of repression.

The second observation relates to another consequence of the confinement of critical histories to the markers, periodization and causal sequencing of linear disciplinary histories. One may wonder what is left of the critical mindset that spearheaded the 'historical turn' and the proliferation of critical

---

181 Theodor W. Adorno, *Negative Dialectics* (Translated by E.B. Ashton) (Routledge, 1973).

182 For another way to address the conservatism of counter-narratives, see Emmanuelle Tourme-Jouannet, "Des Origines Coloniales du Droit International: A Propos du Droit des Gens Moderne au 18ème Siècle", in P.-M. Dupuy and V. Chetail (eds), *The Roots of International Law. Liber Amicorum Peter Haggenmacher* (Nijhoff, 2014), 648, at 670–671.

183 cf Hayden White, *Tropics of Discourse: Essays in Cultural Criticism* (John Hopkins University Press, 1978) 126–127.

histories. In other words, what is actually left of critique in these complacent critical histories? What is the actual space left for critique when the markers, periodization and causal sequencing are the same and equally Eurocentric, leaving no room for the historical imagination of international lawyers? In this respect, it is argued here that the confinement of critical histories to the same markers, periodization and causal sequencing as linear disciplinary histories they seek to disrupt or displace limits the breadth of critique of such works. But this question can even be pushed further. If the works created in the aftermath of the 'historical turn' and the newly enhanced historical self-consciousness of international lawyers are all confined to the same markers, periodization, and causal sequencing as the linear disciplinary histories which were generated at the end of the 19th century and the beginning of the 20th century, one may wonder whether doing history in international law can ever be critical at all?[184] Said differently, could the complacency of critical histories in international law possibly mean there can be no history and no counter-history that is ever critical?

The answer to this question brings the discussion back to the elementary distinction between historicization and historiography made at the start of this article and leads us to a third observation. It is specifically argued here that the type of historiography that has been epitomized by the 'historical turn' cannot be fully critical. Historiography – that is discoursing and theorizing about the specific forms and meanings given to the past by international lawyers and the way in which such past is written – is bound to be reduced to the very terms, vocabularies, and categories of the histories whose writing processes it discusses and hence cannot help upholding dominant markers, periodization and causal sequencing. In other words, whilst historiography helps unearth the "modes of consciousness"[185] as well as the agenda behind the processes of writing history, it cannot evade some degree of rehabilitation of the markers, periodization, and causal sequencing of the linear disciplinary histories whose writing it scrutinizes. In that sense, historiography cannot host radical critique. For the same reason, most of the 'historical turn' in international legal scholarship can be seen as falling short of offering a radical critique.

Following the abovementioned three observations on the incapacity of historiography to host a radical critical attitude, all the elements are now in place to

---

184 cf with Jenkin's idea that history cannot be rescued from historiographical deconstructivism and should not be (Keith Jenkins, *On 'What is History'. From Carr and Elton to Rorty and White* (Roultledge 1995), 79 (Citing Peter Widdowson)).

185 Hayden White, Hayden White, *Metahistory. The Historical Imagination in the 19th-Century Europe* (Johns Hopkins University Press, 2014), 427.

spell out the main argument made in this paper and the idea of radical historical critique. Drawing on the idea that a radical critical attitude cannot be located in historiography, it is argued that the act of history writing can only constitute a radical critique as long as it does away with the markers, periodization and causal sequencing of current histories and renew imagination. In other words, a radical historical critique can only be located in the constant re-writing of previous histories and counter-histories with a view to unburdening[186] historical consciousness of any inherited marker, periodization causal sequencing. Short of such repudiation of the markers, periodization and causal sequencing of current disciplinary histories, critical histories are uncapable of being radically critical. For critical histories to engage in radical historical critique as is understood here, they must move beyond a mere historiographical attitude.[187]

A few indications on what such radical historical critique could look like are in order. In particular, it should be stressed that using old materials in an innovative way[188] falls short of such radical historical critique. As was indicated above, radical historical critique requires a conscious departure from existing and accepted markers, periodization, and causal sequencing. It goes without saying that such radical historical critique cannot be scientific, truth-searching or universalist in character.[189] It does not aim at creating a new totality or intelligibility framework.[190] It only pursues a rupture with the common historical referent of international lawyers' discourses. In this regard, it must be acknowledged that the radical historical critique contemplated here, by disrupting common historical referents of international lawyers' discourses and by rejecting their common markers, periodization, and causal sequencing, come to distort intelligibility frameworks and, thus, bring about unintelligibility in historical discourses. Yet, it is argued here that such unintelligibility should not be feared or taken a dim look at. Indeed, the loss of intelligibility of historical discourses that follows the abandonment of the dominant markers,

---

186 See generally Hayden White, *Metahistory. The Historical Imagination in the 19th-Century Europe* (Johns Hopkins University Press, 2014). On this aspect of Hayden White's work, see Michael S Roth, 'Foreword: "All You've Got is History"' in Hayden White, *Metahistory. The Historical Imagination in the 19th-Century Europe* (JHU Press, 2014) xvii.

187 Comp. with Michel Foucault, *L'archéologie du savoir* (Gallimard, 1969), p. 41 (who argues that once we are freed from immediate forms of continuity, we can start constructing new statements and narratives).

188 This is a plea made by Martti Koskenniemi. See Martti Koskenniemi, 'Histories of International Law: Significance and Problems for a Critical View' [2013] 27 Temple International and Comparative Law Journal 215, 240.

189 See the remarks of Anne Orford against the writing of global history in ibid., 7.

190 Comp. With Theodor W. Adorno, *Negative Dialectics* (Translated by E.B. Ashton) (Routledge, 1973), p. 27

periodization and causal sequencing constitutes a form of disobedience characteristic of radical historical critique.[191]

It must be acknowledged that any new historical narrative that pursues the radical historical critique envisaged here and that does away with the existing markers, periodization and causal sequencing would inevitably come with another set of markers, periodization and causal sequencing that brings about another type of confinement. The critical character comes from the rupture and the radical rewriting irrespective of the possible new confinement it spawns. This also means that radical historical critique is a continuous and never-ending process. Once a disruptive historical narrative has been generated through new markers, periodization and causal sequencing, it will, in turn, be in need of being overturned and rewritten. In that sense, the radical critical histories produced by the radical historical critique contemplated here are bound to be short-lived.[192]

It must also be stressed that those new markers, periodization, and causal sequencing do not necessarily need to be located outside the West or be alien to Europe. In that respect, it is important to highlight that the rupture with common markers, periodization and causal sequencing of the mainstream disciplinary histories that is vindicated here does not *necessarily* need to lead to the production of historical narratives that are entirely alien to Europe and the West. What matters is that these new markers, periodization and causal sequencing displace the markers, periodization and causal sequencing of common disciplinary histories.

The foregoing should suffice to show that the radical historical critique vindicated here does not boil down to the production of counter-histories. It is a new mode of thinking that is not oblivious of the common markers, periodization, and causal sequencing but which registers them with a view to consciously ignoring them in a new space of narrativization.[193] This radical

191 On the idea of disobeying the totality, see T. Adorno, *Positivist Dispute in German Sociology* (Harper Torchbooks, 1976), at 12.

192 See Michel Foucault, *L'archéologie du savoir* (Gallimard, 1969) pp. 44–45 (who argues that, after disrupting existing continuities, we should not be afraid of putting in place new units in our discourses which would need to be disrupted again later).

193 Comp. with Frederic Jameson speaking of Adorno: "What needs to be invented therefore – and what in my opinion Adorno's dialectics proposes – is a new kind of stereoscopic thinking in which the concept continues to be thought philosophically and cashed at face value, while in some part of the mind a very different kind of intellectual regime reigns, a cruder and more sociological set of terms and categories, in which the form of that concept is noted and registered in shorthand and in which the existence of the financial and banking system thereby presupposed is somehow reckoned in". See Frederic Jameson, *Late Marxism. Adorno or the Persistence of the Dialectic* (Verso, 2007), p. 28.

historical critique is interventionist in the sense that it registers accepted markers, periodization and causal sequencing and purposely turns a blind eye thereto. That does not mean, however, that the interventionism at work in the radical historical critique envisaged here can be reduced to an exercise of literary creation. Certainly not. The radical historical critique promoted here – and this is what distinguishes it from dangerous revisionist enterprises – would still need to abide by some elementary empiricism and modes of factual evidence when it comes to the materials that feed into the narrativization concerned. It is true that the modes of evidence and the empiricism informing the establishment of the facts populating the narrativization would themselves be the object of discussion. Yet, the radical critical attitude contemplated here would remain constrained by those – admittedly fluctuating – constraints that apply to any argument for it to be plausible, intelligible, and acceptable for the audience that is the recipient thereof.[194] The foregoing does not mean, however, that radical historical critique ought to be subject to any pre-defined methods or techniques. In particular, for such a radical critique ought to fall short of seeking to substitute a linear, progress, scientific, true, and universal history by another, it shall certainly not espouse any pre-defined mode of investigation that is recognized as properly 'historical'.[195] Rather than a set of methods, the radical historical critique advocated here lies in an attitude geared towards the conscious disruption of the accepted past – and of the common markers, periodization, and causal sequencing along which the latter is shaped – with a view to producing new discourses about international law.

All-in-all, radical historical critique, as is understood here, can be summarized as a conscious political intervention to redraw the past and mobilize it to serve a present claim in a way that deliberately and consciously repudiates existing markers, periodization and causal sequencing. It is argued that there is much to gain from this rupture with the common markers, periodization and causal sequencing of the mainstream disciplinary histories. Radical historical critique in international law as is envisaged here is not about salvaging critique for the sake of critique. It is, more fundamentally, about enabling the production of a wide-range of new discourses about international law itself. In fact, the radical historical critique promoted here would allow international

194 Such rigor is indispensable to avoid radical historical critique falling into disgusting revisionism. Radical historical critique must be very alert to this pitfall.

195 In the same sense, see Anne Orford's plea against the idea that international lawyers should embrace "historical methods", see Anne Orford, 'On international legal method' [2013] 1 London Review of International Law 166. See also Anne Orford, 'International Law and the Limits of History' in W Werner and others (eds), *The Law of International Lawyers: Reading Martti Koskenniemi* (CUP 2015) 302–303 and 312.

lawyers to imagine new contexts, new places, and new moments where legal claims and legal practices are made and unmade. In that sense, writing radical critical histories is about telling new stories filled with new actors, new turning points, new moments of rupture, new causations, new revolutionary moments, new agendas, new revolutions, new watershed moments, new turning points, new points of rupture, new crises, new revolutionary moments, new infidelities, new milestones, new beginning, new ends, new transitional periods, new genealogies, new pedigrees, new modes of liberation, new legal concepts, and new thoughts. Whilst these new stories would inevitably remain informed by the totality of the idea of international law itself, the rupture with the common markers, periodization, and causal sequencing and the production of new contexts, new places, and new moments would allow international lawyers, not only to better apprehend the hidden works of the totality of international law, but also to enable the production of new discourses about international law itself.

6 Concluding Remarks

International lawyers have long been endowed with historical self-consciousness and proved historians of sorts. Following the 'historical turn' – which has been understood here as a turn to historiography – international lawyers discovered the virtues of historiographical inquiries and turned themselves into historiographers of sorts. This historical turn has buoyed rich and prolific historiographical discussions that have led to very insightful and welcome questioning of the dominant linear disciplinary histories of the field. Yet, as has been pointed out here, these new scholarly studies have proved complacent because of their perpetuating the markers, periodization and causal sequencing of these dominant linear disciplinary histories. It has been argued that radical historical critique requires a conscious and interventionist history-writing that disrupts existing markers, periodization and causal sequencing of the accepted disciplinary histories. At this ultimate stage of the discussion, three observations are still warranted with respect to some of the epistemological consequences on the idea of radical historical critique and thus the type of critical attitude advocated in this article.

A first observation pertains to the consequences of radical historical critique for international law as an autonomous discipline organized around some key self-sustained truth-claims and paradigms. As was indicated in the introduction above, disciplinary history is indispensable for the legitimacy and acceptability of the truth-claims that regulate interpretation and discourses within the discipline. Disciplinary history is also instrumental in the self-awareness of those actors constituting the discipline that they are agents of a disciplinary project. The idea of radical historical critique defended here begs the question whether doing away with the markers, periodization, and causal sequencing of the common histories of international law as is entailed by the radical historical critique advocated here jeopardizes the truth-claims as well as the identity of the discipline which such histories sustain. Said differently, one may wonder whether radical historical critique imperil the key paradigms and fundamental doctrines constitutive of international law as a discipline. It is argued at this concluding stage that the risk of a loss of disciplinary autonomy should not be exaggerated. Radical historical critique as is envisaged here is not meant to deprive the discipline from any disciplinary history but rather to ensure that disciplinary histories are renewed constantly. What is more, the radical historical critique advocated here, even if it is accompanied by a distortion of intelligibility frameworks, is not necessarily meant to repudiate and disable the truth-claims and paradigms of the discipline but only to shed a new light thereon. It could even be argued that international lawyers engaged in a conscious history-rewriting as is defended here are necessarily guided by the truth-claim and paradigms which they have been trained to deploy and respond to and which they will accordingly uphold in their radical historical critique. In that sense, the radical historical critique proposed here ought not to bring about a loss of disciplinary autonomy and identity.

This resilience of the disciplinary autonomy and identity in spite of the radical historical critique is further confirmed by the extent to which international lawyers' engagement with history continues to be fundamentally distinct from history as a discipline.[196] This is the object of a second concluding observation that relates to the distinction between (international) law and (international) history. It is commonly assumed that the distinction between law and history has been inherited from modernity.[197] This modern distinction

196 History as a discipline is what Janne Nijman has called "history for history's sake" that is an allegedly a-theoretical and a-functional engagement with the past. See Janne Nijman, Seeking Change by Doing History (April 24, 2018). Seeking Change by Doing History (Amsterdam University Press, 2018), 25 Pp. Available at SSRN: https://ssrn.com/abstract=3167708, pp. 7–9. See gen. Keith Jenkins, Re-thinking History (Routledge, 2003), at 82: "In liberal discourse there is always posited, somewhere and somehow, a sort of neutral ground from which it looks precisely as if you can choose or not. This neutral ground is not seen as another position one already occupies, but is considered rather as a disinterested site from which one can sit back and objectively make unbiased choices and judgements".

197 See e.g. Anne Orford, "The Past as Law of History? The Relevance of Imperialism for Modern International Law" IILJ Working Papers 2012/2 History and Theory of

has however been played down by both critical historians[198] as well as critical legal scholars[199] over the last decades, many of them contending that historical and legal discourses boil down to a similar mobilization of a past which is organized in the present with a view to serving the future.[200] The radical historical critique advocated in this article and whereby international lawyers are encouraged to consciously rewrite their histories could be construed as further belittling the distinction between history and international law. This belittling of the distinction between history and international law raises the question whether it remains possible to distinguish international law and history at all. It is argued here that despite international law and history sharing a similar mobilization of the past, they remain distinct. Not only are international lawyers engaging with history-writing through the deployment of a very different conceptual apparatus. International lawyers also do so according to methods, modes of inquiry and discursive techniques that ought not to be congruent with those accepted in the discipline of History.[201] This is even more so with respect to the radical historical critique advocated here which is geared

---

International Law Series, p. 8. See however Harold J. Berman, *Law and Revolution. The Formation of the Western Legal Tradition* (Harvard University Press, 1983). He argues that the distinction between law and other disciplines as well as social institutions originated in the differentiation of the ecclesiastical polity and secular polities during the Investiture Struggle (1075–1122) and the Papal revolution in the 11th and 12th century

198 Comp with Hayden White, Tropics of Discourse, pp. 126–127; Hayden White, Metahistory. The Historical Imagination in the 19th-Century Europe (Johns Hopkins University Press, 2014), at 428; Keith Jenkins, On 'What is History'. From Carr and Elton to Rorty and White (Roultledge, 1995), p. 65 and 82.

199 Christopher N. Warren, "History, Literature, and Authority in International Law", in Maksymilian Del Mar, Bernadette Meyler, and Simon Stern (eds), Oxford Handbook of Law and Humanities (OUP, forthcoming); see also A. Orford, International Law and the Limits of History, in W. Werner, A. Galán, and M. de Hoon (eds), The Law of International Lawyers: Reading Martti Koskenniemi (CUP August 2015), at 297–320, at 311 (citing C. Fasolt, The Limits of History (University of Chicago Press, 2004). See the remarks of Marti Koskenniemi, in Alexandra Kemmerer, "We do not need to always look to Westphalia … A Conversation with Martti Koskenniemi and Anne Orford", 17 Journal of the History of International Law (2015) 1–14, at p. 9. Comp with the plea of Janne Nijman for the study of history and international law together, that is what she calls "History for self-knowledge" (Janne Nijman, Seeking Change by Doing History (April 24, 2018). Seeking Change by Doing History (Amsterdam University Press, 2018), 25 Pp. Available at SSRN: https://ssrn.com/abstract=3167708, pp. 10–13).

200 See gen. R. Barthes, Mythologies, Editions du Seuil, 1957, p. 215 : « plus un système est spécifiquement défini dans ses formes, et plus il est docile à la critique historique. Parodiant un mot connu, je dirai qu'un peu de formalisme éloigne de l'Histoire, mais beaucoup y ramène ».

201 Anne Orford, 'International Law and the Limits of History' in W Werner and others (eds), *The Law of International Lawyers: Reading Martti Koskenniemi* (CUP 2015) 297, at 312.

towards interventionist history-rewriting short of any pre-agreed methods. In that sense, the radical historical critique advocated, although it draws on the fundamental historicizing character of legal thought and practice, can be seen as buoying the disciplinary specificity of international lawyers' engagement with the past, further distinguishing international legal thought and practice from the discipline of History.

The argument has been made above that radical historical critique comes with no predefined set of methods or techniques, let alone requires the resort to modes of inquiry practiced in the discipline of History. Does this mean that no disciplinary constraints apply to those engaging in radical historical critique in international law? In other words, is the entitlement to engage in radical historical critique and, thus, in conscious interventionist history rewriting, dependent on certain credentials, skills, affiliations, or origin? This question is the object of a third and final observation which pertains to the entitlement to engage in radical historical critique. In this regard, it is preliminarily contended that the common social constraints that apply to the production of any international legal discourse continue to apply to the production of radical historical critique as is understood here. Indeed, radical historical critique is just another type of legal discourse that mobilizes and organizes the past. Like any legal discourse, radical historical critique must meet those constraints – and thus also the requirements of the disciplinary truth-claims – which are held determinative of the plausibility and authority of all legal discourses in the field. This includes a certain degree of seriousness in the treatment and referencing of one's sources and materials. Yet, because radical historical critique entails the conscious and interventionist rewriting of historical narratives, one may wonder whether the rewriting of historical narratives and the departure from the common markers, periodization and causal sequencing can be left open to any international lawyers wherever she or he comes from or wherever she or he is located. More specifically, one may wonder whether there are geographical constraints on the entitlement to flout markers, periodization, and causal sequencing and engage in radical historical critique as is understood here. For instance, and said very concretely, can a European scholar rewrite historical narratives whose main markers, periodization, or causal sequencing are located in non-European locations? And, conversely, can a non-European scholar rewrite historical narratives whose main markers, periodization, or causal sequencing are located in a European location? At this ultimate stage of the discussion, it is argued here that no such geographical or cultural constraints (should) apply to radical historical critique advocated here. Any international lawyer can engage in conscious and interventionist rewriting of historical narratives about international law whatever the markers, periodization, and causal sequencing subject to radical historical critique are and whatever her or his location. This is so because no location has any universal history of its own, let alone belongs to any specific geographical and cultural group of international lawyers. As was pointed out, radical historical critique in international law as is understood here does not pursue any historical necessity or universality. It is true that, in international law, geographical proximity between the author of radical historical critique and the location of the markers, periodization, and causal sequencing under scrutiny impinge on the authority and persuasiveness of the new historical narrative so produced. It is also true that there are important material and linguistic obstacles to a rewriting of history in locations foreign to the author of the radical historical critique.[202] Although such material and linguistic obstacles should not be played down or treated lightly, they are not insurmountable. And they certainly do not justify any principled requirement of geographical or cultural proximity between the location of the author of radical historical critique and the location of the markers, periodization and causal sequencing under scrutiny. Such principled requirement of geographical or cultural proximity would most likely stifle the critical thrust of any radical historical critique as is envisaged here. It could even be argued that, provided that the highest rigor is applied in terms of sources and argumentation, the larger the geographical or cultural distance between the location of the author of the radical historical critique and the location of the markers, periodization and causal sequencing under scrutiny is, the sharper the radical historical critique could potentially prove. At the end of the day, given the Westcentricism of the dominant markers, periodization, and causal sequencing of the dominant histories of international law, the greatest potential for a renewal of the historical narratives about international law that do away with the markers, periodization, and causal sequencing of the dominant histories of international law – and thus the greatest potential for a critical attitude in the history of international law as has been construed in this article – will probably be found outside the Western circles of the discipline.

202 See the remarks of Maiko Meguro, "Backlash against international law by the East? How the concept of 'transplantation' helps us to better understand reception processes of international law", Völkerrechtsblog, 11 January 2019, available at https://voelkerrechtsblog.org/backlash-against-international-law-by-the-east/.

Bibliography

Adorno, Theodor W., *Negative Dialectics* (Translated by E.B. Ashton) (Routledge, 1973).

Adorno, Theodor W., *Positivist Dispute in German Sociology* (Harper Torchbooks 1976).

Alasdair MacIntyre, *After Virtue: A Study in Moral Theory* (3rd ed, Duckworth 2007).

Alexandrowicz, Charles Henry, 'Grotius and India' reproduced in C.H. Alexandrowicz, *The Law of Nations in Global History* (OUP 2017).

Alexandrowicz, Charles Henry, *An Introduction to the History of the Law of Nations in the East Indies* (Clarendon 1967).

Alexandrowicz, Charles Henry, *The Law of Nations in Global History* (OUP 2017).

Allott, Philip, 'Language, Method and the Nature of International Law' [1971] 45 *British Yearbook of International* Law 79, 122.

Anand, Ram Prakash, *'Origin and Development of the Law of the Sea: History of International Law Revisited'* (Martinus Nijhoff, 1983).

Anghie, Antony, 'The Evolution of International Law: colonial and postcolonial realities' (2006) 27 (5) *Third World Quarterly* 739–753.

Anghie, Antony, *Imperialism, Sovereignty and the Making of International Law* (CUP 2004).

Arendt, Hannah, *On Violence* (Houghton Mifflin Harcourt 1970) 237–238.

Arendt, Hannah, *Origins of Totalitarianism* (Schocken Books 1951).

Armitage, David and Jennifer Pitts, "'This Modern Grotius': An Introduction to the Life and Thought of C.H. Alexandrowicz", in Charles Henry Alexandrowicz, *The Law of Nations in Global History* (OUP, 2017).

Armitage, David, "The Fifty Years' Rift: Intellectual History and International Relations" 1 *Modern Intellectual History* (2004) 97–109.

Banu, Roxana, *Nineteenth-Century Perspectives on Private International Law* (OUP, 2018).

Barreto, José-Manuel, 'Cerberus: Rethinking Grotius and the Westphalian System' in Martti Koskenniemi, Walter Rech, and Manuel Jimenez Fonseca (eds), *International Law and Empire* (OUP 2017).

Barreto, Manuel, 'Cerberus: Rethinking Grotius and the Westphalian System' in Martti Koskenniemi, Walter Rech, and Manuel Jimenez Fonseca (eds), *International Law and Empire* (OUP, 2017) 152–154.

Barthes, Roland, 'le discours de l'histoire' (1967) 6 (4) *Social Science Information* 63, 74.

Barthes, Roland, *Le degré zéro de l'écriture, Editions du Seuil*, 1972.

Bederman, David J., *International Law in Antiquity* (CUP 2004).

Bell, Duncan, "International Relations: The Dawn of a Historiographical Turn?" 3 *British Journal of Politics and International Relations* (2001) 115–126.

Bentley, Jerry H., 'Cross- Cultural Interaction and Periodization in World History' (1996) 101(3) *American Historical Review* 749–770.

Benton, Lauren, 'Made in Empire: Finding the History of International Law in Imperial Locations', 31 *Leiden Journal of International Law* (2018) 473–478.

Berman, Harold J., *Law and Revolution. The Formation of the Western Legal Tradition* (Harvard University Press, 1983).

Berman, Nathaniel, In the Wake of Empire 14 *American University International Law Review* (1999) 1521–1554.

Besserman, Lee, *The Challenge of Periodization: Old Paradigms and New Perspectives* (Garland Publishing 1996).

Brierly, James Leslie, The Law of Nations. An Introduction to the International Law of Peace (6th ed. Clarendon Press 1963).

Brown, Chris, Terry Nardin, and Nicholas Rengger, eds., *International Relations in Political Thought: Texts from the Ancient Greeks to the First World War* (CUP 2002).

Brown, Marshall, 'Periods and Resistance', (2001) 62 (4) *Modern Language Quarterly* 309–316.

Butler, Judith, 'Critically Queer' (1993) 1 (1) *Journal of Lesbian and Gay Studies* 17–32.

Carr, Edward Hallet, *What is History?* (2nd ed, CUP 1987).

Carty, Anthony, 'Interwar German Theories of International Law: The Psychoanalytical and Phenomenological Perspectives of Hans Kelsen and Carl Schmitt' (1995) 16 (2) *Cardozo Law Review* 1235–1292.

Cass, Deborah Z., 'Navigating the Newstream: Recent Critical Scholarship in International Law' (1996) 65 (3) *Nordic Journal of International Law* 47–90.

Chimni, BS, 'Third World Approaches to International Law: A Manifesto' (2006) 8 *International Community Law Review* 3.

Chimni, BS, *International Law and World Order. A Critique of Contemporary Approaches* (2nd ed, CUP 2017).

Chimini, BS, 'The Past, Present, and Future of International Law: A Critical Third World Approach' 8 *Melbourne Journal of International Law* 499.

Coates, Benjamin Allen, *Legalist Empire. International Law and American Foreign Relations in the Early Twentieth Century* (OUP, 2016).

Cohen, Harlan Grant, 'Are We (Americans) All International Legal Realists Now?' in Chiara Giorgetti and Guglielmo Verdirame (eds), *Concepts on International Law in Europe and the United States* (Cambridge University Press, Forthcoming).

Craven, Matthew 'Introduction: International Law and Its Histories in Matthew Craven' in M Fitzmaurice and M Vogiatzi (eds) *Time, History and International Law* (Brill 2007).

Craven, Matthew, 'The Invention of a Tradition: Westlake, The Berlin Conference and the Historicisation of International Law' in Luigi Nuzzo and Miloš Vec *Constructing International Law: The Birth of a Discipline* (Klostermann 2012).

Craven, Mathew, 'Theorizing the Turn to History in International Law', in Anne Orford and Florian Hoffmann (eds), *The Oxford Handbook of the Theory of International Law* (OUP 2016).

d'Aspremont, Jean, 'Bindingness' in J d'Aspremont and S Singh (eds), *Fundamental Concepts for International Law: The Construction of a Discipline* (Elgar 2016).

d'Aspremont, Jean, 'Martti Koskenniemi, the Mainstream, and Self-Reflectivity' (2016) 29 *Leiden Journal of International Law* 625–639.

d'Aspremont, Jean, *International Law as a Belief System* (CUP, 2017).

d'Aspremont, Jean, International Lawyers and Legal Forms: Transatlantic Denials, Forthcoming in Chiara Giorgetti & Guglielmo Verdirame (eds), *Concepts on International Law in Europe and the United States* (Cambridge University Press, forthcoming).

d'Aspremont, Jean, The professionalization of international law in Jean d'Aspremont and others, *International Law as Profession* (CUP 2017).

Davis, Kathleen, *Periodization and Sovereignty: How Ideas of Feudalism and Secularization Govern the Politics of Time* (University of Philadelphia Press 2008).

de la Rasilla del Moral, Ignacio, 'The Ambivalent Shadow of the Pre-Wilsonian Rise of International Law' (2014) 7 *Erasmus Law Review* 2.

De Lapradelle, Albert Geouffre, *De la nationalité d'origine, droit compare, droit interne, droit international* (A Giard & E Brièr 1893).

de Visscher, Charles, *Théories et Réalités en Droit International Public* (4th ed., Pedone, 1970).

Diggelman, Oliver, 'The Periodization of the History of International Law' in Bardo Fassbender and Anne Peters (eds), *The Oxford Handbook of the History of International Law* (OUP, 2012).

Dunne, Tim, Inventing International Society: A History of the English School (Macmillan 1998).

Elías, Taslim Olawale, *Africa and the Development of International Law* (Sijthoff 1972).

Eslava, Luis, Michael Fakhri, and Vasuki Nesiah, Bandung, *Global History and International Law. Critical Pasts and Pending Futures* (CUP 2017).

Fassbender, Bardo, 'Peace of Westphalia (1648)' *Max Planck Encyclopedia of Public International Law* (2011).

Fitzmaurice, Andrew, 'Liberalism and Empire in Nineteenth-Century International Law' (2012) 117 (1) *American Historical Review* 122–140.

Foucault, Michel, *L'archéologie du savoir* (Gallimard 1969).

Galindo, George Rodrigo Bandeira, 'Martti Koskenniemi and the Historiographical Turn in International Law' (2005) 16 *European Journal of International Law* 539–559.

Garcia-Salmones Rovira, Monica, *The Project of Positivism in International Law* (OUP 2013).

Green, William A., 'Periodizing World History' (1995) 34 (2) *History and Theory* 99–111.

Grewe, Wilhelm, *The epochs of international law* (Walter de Gruyter 2000).

Gross, Leo, 'The Peace of Westphalia, 1648–1948' (1948) 42 *American Journal of International Law* 29.

Guggenheim, Paul, "Les Origines de la Notion autonome du Droit des Gens", in *Symbolae Verzijl* (Nijhoff, 1958).

Hamamoto, Shotaro, 'A propose de deux clichés sur l'histoire du droit international en Asie de l'Est : une reconsidération de l'ordre mondial chinois et du discours de traités inégaux' in in P.-M. Dupuy and V. Chetail (eds), *The Roots of International Law. Liber Amicorum Peter Haggenmacher* (Nijhoff, 2014).

Haskell, John, 'Hugo Grotius in the Contemporary Memory of International Law: Secularism, Liberalism, and the Politics of Restatement and Denial' in J M Beneyto, D Kennedy, J Corti Varela and J Haskell (eds.) *New approaches to international law: the European and the American experiences* (Asser Press 2012).

Haskell, John, 'The Traditions of Modernity within International Law and Governance: Christianity, Liberalism, and Marxism' (2014) 6 *Human Rights & Globalization Law Review* 29.

Hathaway, Oona A. and Scott J. Shapiro, *The Internationalists. How a Radical Plan to Outlaw War Remade the World* (Simon & Schuster 2017).

Hobsbawm, Eric, 'Introduction: inventing traditions' in E Hobsbawm and T Ranger (eds), *The Invention of Tradition* (CUP 1983) 1–14.

Jameson, Frederic, *Late Marxism. Adorno or the Persistence of the Dialectic* (Verso, 2007).

Jeffery, Renee, *Hugo Grotius in International Thought* (Palgrave Macmillan 2006).

Jenkins, Keith, *Re-thinking History* (Routledge 2003) 7.

Jenkins, Keith, *On 'What is History'. From Carr and Elton to Rorty and White* (Roultledge 1995) 6.

Kemmerer, Alexandra, 'We do not need to always look to Westphalia … A Conversation with Martti Koskenniemi and Anne Orford' [2015] 17 Journal of the History of International Law.

Kennedy, Duncan, 'Primitive Legal Scholarship' [1986] 27 *Harvard International Law Journal* 1–98.

Kennedy, Duncan, 'International Law and the Nineteenth Century: History of an Illusion' (1996) 17 *QLR* 99.

Kennedy, Duncan, 'The Sources of International Law' (1987) 2 (1) *American University International Law Review* 1.

Kleinlein, Thomas, 'International Legal Thought: Creation of a Tradition and the Potential of Disciplinary Self-Reflection' in Giuliana Ziccardi Capaldo, *The Global Community: Yearbook of International Law and Jurisprudence 2016* (OUP 2016) 811, 816.

Kleinlein, Thomas, 'International Legal Thought: Creation of a Tradition and the Potential of Disciplinary Self-Reflection' in Giuliana Ziccardi Capaldo, *The Global Community: Yearbook of International Law and Jurisprudence 2016* (OUP 2016).

Kochi, Tarik, *The Other's War. Recognition and the Violence of Ethics* (Birkbeck Law Press 2009).

Kolb, Robert, "Considérations sur le droit international public des anciennes cultures extra-européennes", in P.-M. Dupuy and V. Chetail (eds), *The Roots of International Law. Liber Amicorum Peter Haggenmacher* (Nijhoff, 2014) 673–709.

Koselleck, Reinhart, 'On the Need for Theory in the Discipline of History' in Koselleck, *The Practice of Conceptual History*, 4.

Koselleck, Reinhart, *The Practice of Conceptual History* (Stanford University Press 2002).

Koskenniemi, Martti, 'Lauterpacht: The Victorian Tradition in International Law' 8 (2) *European Journal of International Law* 215, 261.

Koskenniemi, Martti, *Gentle Civilizer of Nations* (Cambridge University Press 2001).

Koskenniemi, Martti, 'Introduction: International Law and Empire – Aspects and Approaches' in Martti Koskenniemi, Walter Rech, and Manuel Jimenez Fonseca (eds), *International Law and Empire* (OUP 2017) 4.

Koskenniemi, Martti, 'Epilogue' in W Werner and others, *The Law of International Lawyers. Reading Martti Koskenniemi* (CUP 2017).

Koskenniemi, Martti, 'Histories of International Law: Dealing with Eurocentrism', lecture on 16 November 2011, 5.

Koskenniemi, Martti, 'Histories of International Law: Significance and Problems for a Critical View' (2013) 27 *Temple International and Comparative Law Journal* 215.

Koskenniemi, Martti, 'Into Positivism: Georg Friedrich von Martens (1756–1821) and Modern International Law' (2008) 15 *Constellations* 189–207.

Koskenniemi, Martti, "International Law and the Emergence of Mercantile Capitalism: Grotius To Smith" in P.-M. Dupuy and V. Chetail (eds), *The Roots of International Law. Liber Amicorum Peter Haggenmacher* (Nijhoff, 2014) 3.

Koskenniemi, Martti, The Case for Comparative International Law, 20 *Finnish Yearbook of International Law* (2009).

Laghmani, Slim, "Les Origines du droit international public et le concept de discours fondateur", in in P.-M. Dupuy and V. Chetail (eds), *The Roots of International Law. Liber Amicorum Peter Haggenmacher* (Nijhoff, 2014).

Lange, Felix, 'The dream of a völkish colonial empire: international law and colonial law during the National Socialist era' (2017) 4 (3) *London Review of International Law* 343–369.

Laurent, François, *Histoires du droit des gens et des relations internationales* (Lelong, 18 volumes).

Lauterpacht, Hersch, 'International Law after the Convenant' in *International Law Collected Papers 2. The Law of the Peace, Part I International Law in General* (CUP 1975).

Lauterpacht, Hersch, 'The Grotian Tradition in International Law' (1946) 23 The British Yearbook of International Law 1, 18–19.

Lauterpacht, Hersch, *Oppenheim's International Law* (8th edition, Longman 1955).

Lauterpacht, Hersch, *The Function of Law in the International Community* (2nd edition, OUP 2011) 95.

Lesaffer, Randall, 'International Law and Its History: The Story of an Unrequited Love' in Matthew Craven, Malgosia Fitzmaurice and Maria Vogiatzi (eds), *Time, History and International Law* (Brill 2007).

Lesaffer, Randall, 'The classical law of nations (1500–1800)' in A Orakhelashvili (ed), *Research Handbook on the Theory and History of International Law* (Elgar 2011).

Lesaffer, Randall, 'The Grotian Tradition Revisited: Change and Continuity in the History of International Law' (2003) 73 (1) *British Yearbook of International Law* (2002) 103, 137.

Lev, Amnon, 'The transformation of international law in the 19th century' in A Orakhelashvili (ed), *Research Handbook on the Theory and History of International Law* (Elgar 2011).

Levi-Strauss, Claude, *The Savage Mind* (University of Chicago Press 1966).

Lobban, Michael, 'English Approaches to International Law in the Nineteenth Century' in Ma Craven, M Fitzmaurice and M Vogiatzi (eds) *Time, History and International Law* (Brill 2007).

Lorca, Arnulf Becker, Eurocentricism in the History of International Law, in Bardo Fassbender and Anne Peters (eds), *The Oxford Handbook of the History of International Law* (OUP, 2012).

Lorca, Arnulf Becker, *Mestizo International Law: A Global Intellectual History 1841–1933* (CUP 2014).

Meguro, Maiko, "Backlash against international law by the East? How the concept of 'transplantation' helps us to better understand reception processes of international law", Völkerrechtsblog (11 January 2019) available at https://voelkerrechtsblog.org/backlash-against-international-law-by-the-east/ (accessed 8 May 2019).

Miéville, China, *Between Equal Rights: A Marxist Theory of International Law* (Haymarket Books 2006).

Mills, Alex, 'The Private History of International Law' (2006) 55 *International & Comparative Law Quarterly* 1–50.

Munslow, Alun, 'Preface' in Keith Jenkins, *On 'What is History'. From Carr and Elton to Rorty and White* (Roultledge 1995).

Mutua, Makau, 'Savages, Victims and Saviors: The Metaphor of Human Rights' (2001) 42 (1) *Harvard International Law Journal* 201.

Mutua, Makau, 'What is TWAIL?' 94 *American Society of International Law Proceedings* 31.

Neff, Stephen, *Justice Among Nations. A History of International Law* (Harvard University Press, 2014).

Nijman, Janne, Seeking Change by Doing History (April 24, 2018). Seeking Change by Doing History (Amsterdam University Press, 2018), 25 Available at SSRN: https://ssrn.com/abstract=3167708).

Nuzzo, Luigi, "The Birth of an Imperial Location: Comparative Perspectives on Western Colonialism in China" 31 *Leiden Journal of International Law* (2018) 569–596.

Nys, Ernest, *Les origines du droit international* (Castaigne, 1894).

Obregon, Liliana, 'Marti Koskenniemi's Critique of Eurocentricism in International Law', in A Galan, M de Hoon, and W Werner (eds), *The Law of International Lawyers: Reading Martti Koskenniemi* (CUP, 2017).

Obregon, Liliana, 'Writing International Legal History: An Overview', (2015) 7 *Monde(s)* 95, 110.

Obregon, Liliana, "Empire, Racial Capitalism and International Law: The Case of Manumitted Haiti and the Recognition Debt", (2018) 31 *Leiden Journal of International Law* 597–615.

Onuma, Yasuaki, 'When Was the Law of International Society Born – An Inquiry of the History of International Law from an Intercivilizational Perspective', 2 *Journal of History of International Law* (2000) 1–66.

Onuma, Yasuaki, *International Law in a Transcivilizational World* (CUP 2017).

Oppenheim, Lassa Francis Lawrence, 'The Science of International Law: Its Task and Method' (1908) 2 (2) *American Journal of International Law* 93–356.

Orakhelashvili, Alexander, 'The relevance of theory and history – the essence and origins of international law' in A Orakhelashvili (ed), *Research Handbook on the Theory and History of International Law* (Elgar 2011).

Orford, Anne, 'On international legal method' [2013] 1 *London Review of International Law* 166–197.

Orford, Anne, 'Scientific Reason and the Discipline of International Law' (2014) 25 *European Journal of International Law* 166–197.

Orford, Anne, 'The Past as Law of History? The Relevance of Imperialism for Modern International Law' (2012) U of Melbourne Legal Studies Research Paper 600, 608 <https://papers.ssrn.com/sol3/papers.cfm?abstract_id=2090434> accessed 14 June 2018.

Osiander, Andreas, 'Sovereignty, 'International Relations, and the Westphalian Myth' (2001) 55 (2) *International Organization* 251–287.

Pahuja, Sundhya, "The Postcoloniality of International Law" 46 *Harvard International Law Journal* (2005).

Parfitt, Rose, 'The Spectre of Sources' (2014) 25 *European Journal of International Law* 297, 298.

Perreau-Saussine, Amanda, 'A Case Study on Jurisprudence as a Source of International Law: Oppenheim's Influence' in Matthew Craven, Malgosia Fitzmaurice and Maria Vogiatzi (eds), *Time, History and International Law* (Brill 2007).

Pillet, Allan (ed), *Les Fondateurs du Droit International* (Giard et Brière, 1904).

Preiser, Wolfgang, 'History of International Law, Basic Questions and Principles' Max Planck Encyclopedia of Public International Law (2007).

Purcell, Kate, 'Faltering at the Critical Turn to History: 'Juridical Thinking' in International Law and Genealogy as History, Critique, and Therapy' (2016) Jean Monnet Working Paper Series, JMWP 02/15.

Rech, Walter, 'International Law, Empire, and the Relative Indeterminacy of Narrative' in Martti Koskenniemi, Walter Rech, and Manuel Jimenez Fonseca (eds), *International Law and Empire* (OUP 2017).

Ricoeur, Paul, '*Time and Narative*' (Chicago University Press, 1983).

Rockmore T., 'Hegel' in Aviezer Tucker (ed), *A Companion to the Philosophy of History and Historiography* (Wiley-Blackwell 2011).

Rolin, Henri, « Notice sur Ernest Nys » (1951–1952) 4 *Revue de l'Université de Bruxelles* 349–357.

Roth, Michael S., 'Foreword: "All You've Got is History"' in Hayden White, *Metahistory. The Historical Imagination in the 19th-Century Europe* (JHU Press 2014).

Said, Edward, *Orientalism* (Routledge 1978).

Salmon, Jean, « notice Ernest Nys », Nouvelle biographie nationale, (2007) 9 *Académie royale de Belgique.*

Scarfi, Juan Pablo, *The Hidden History of International Law in the Americas. Empire and Legal Networks* (OUP 2017).

Schlag, Pierre, '"Le Hors de Texte, C'est Moi" The Politics of Form and the Domestication of Deconstruction' (1990) 11 *Cardozo Law Review* 133–176.

Schmidt, Brian, *The Political Discourse of Anarchy: A Disciplinary History of International Relations* (State University of New York Press 1998).

Shahabuddin, Mohammad, "The 'standard of civilization' in international law: Intellectual perspectives from pre-war Japan" 32 *Leiden Journal of International Law* (2019) 13–32.

Simpson, Gerry, *Great Powers and Outlaw States. Unequal Sovereigns in their International Legal Order* (CUP, 2004).

Skouteris, Thomas, 'The Sources of International Law: Tales of Progress' (2000) *Hague Yearbook of International Law* 11–17.

Southgate, Beverley, 'Postmodernism' in Aviezer Tucker (ed), *A Companion to the Philosophy of History and Historiography* (Wiley-Blackwell, 2011).

Spiermann, Ole, *International Legal Argument in the Permanent Court of International Justice: The Rise of International Judiciary* (CUP 2005).

Stearns, Peter, 'Periodization in World History Teaching' (1987) 20 (4) *History Teacher* 561–580.

Steiger, Heinhard, 'From the International Law of Christianity to the International Law of the World Citizens' (2001) 3 *Journal of the History of International* Law 180–193.

Straumann, Benjamin, '"Ancient Caesarean Lawyers" in a State of Nature: Roman Tradition and Natural Rights in Hugo Grotius's "De iure praedae"' (2006) 34 *Political Theory* 133–155.

Strauss, Claude Levi, 'The Structural Study of Myth' (1955) 68 (270) *The Journal of American Floklore* 428.

Surkis, Judith, 'When Was the Linguistic Turn? A Genealogy' (2012) 117 (3) *American Historical Review* 700, 701.

Tourme-Jouannet, Emmanuelle, 'Universalism and Imperialism: The True-False Paradox of International Law?' (2007) 18 (3) *European Journal of International Law* 479–407.

Tourme-Jouannet, Emmanuelle, "Des Origines Coloniales du Droit International : A Propos du Droit des Gens Moderne au 18ème Siècle" in P.-M. Dupuy and V. Chetail (eds) *The Roots of International Law. Liber Amicorum Peter Haggenmacher* (Nijhoff 2014).

Tucker, Aviezer, 'Introduction' in Aviezer Tucker (ed), *A Companion to the Philosophy of History and Historiography* (Wiley-Blackwell 2011).

Venzke, Ingo, 'What If? Counterfactual (Hi)Stories of International Law' (2016) 8 (2) *Asian Journal of International Law* 403–431.

Ward, Robert Plumer, *An Enquiry into the Foundation and History of the Law of Nations, from the Time of the Greeks and Romans to the Age of Grotius* (Strahan and Woodfall 1795).

Warren, Christopher N., 'History, Literature, and Authority in International Law' in Maksymilian Del Mar, Bernadette Meyler, and Simon Stern (eds), *Oxford Handbook of Law and Humanities* (OUP, forthcoming).

Werner, Wouter, Marieke de Hoon and Alexis Galán (eds.)*The Law of International Lawyers: Reading Martti Koskenniemi* (CUP 2015).

White, Hayden, 'The Question of Narrative in Contemporary Historical Theory' (1984) 23 (1) *History and Theory* 1–33.

White, Hayden, 'Historical Discourse and Literary Writing' in Kuisma Korhonen (ed) *Tropes for the Past: Hayden White and the History/Literature Debate* (Rodopi 2006).

White, Hayden, *Metahistory. The Historical Imagination in the 19th-Century Europe* (Johns Hopkins University Press, 2014).

White, Hayden, *Tropics of Discourse: Essays in Cultural Criticism* (John Hopkins University Press, 1978).

Wijffels, Alain, 'Early-modern scholarship on international law' in A Orakhelashvili (ed), *Research Handbook on the Theory and History of International Law* (Elgar 2011).

Wilder, Gary, 'From Optic to Topic: The Foreclosure Effect of Historiographic Turns' (2012) 117 (3) *American Historical Review* 723–745.